JOSEPH ⌣⎽⎽⎽

A Practical Guide to Traditional Astrology

Publications

Published by the

Archive for the Retrieval of Historical Astrological Texts
a division of Arhat Media Inc.
P.O. Box 2008 Reston, VA 20195
www.robhand.com

Table of Contents

Introduction

This book began as a series of articles published by *The Mountain Astrologer* in 1995 and 1996. In this book I explain to the modern astrologer some of the best ideas and techniques from the natal astrology of the past. You can apply this information to your natal chart and the charts of others to gain new insights and methods. I also hope that you will use it to learn more about the origin of astrology, its history and potential.

This booklet is truly a community effort. The staff of The *Mountain Astrologer* provided the initial context. The translations and commentaries of Robert Hand, Robert Schmidt and Robert Zoller provided its foundations. Geraldine Hanlon lent editorial assistance, particularly on the first and last chapters. My wife, Jill-laurie Crane, had the initial idea for the project and patiently endured its process. Editorial help was provided by Bonnie Brugger as well as my astrological best friends, Marcia Butchart, Dorian Greenbaum, and Priscilla Harlan.

As a modern astrologer I conduct a private practice using modern astrology; I also teach modern astrology to beginning students up to budding professionals. Over the past five years, however, traditional ideas and techniques have influenced my natal work. My purpose is not to replace one style of astrology with another but to reclaim and promote the richness of traditional and modern astrology together.

"Traditional astrology" is not one school or set of ideas but constitutes fifteen hundred years of changing assumptions and cultural contexts. In this book we'll focus on ideas from the late Hellenistic period and the style of astrology that flourished in Europe from the 1100's to about 1700.

In Chapter 1 we'll see how astrologers from ancient and medieval times used signs to depict the *essential dignity or debility* of a planet. In Chapter 2 on *houses* you will read that in Hellenistic astrology the signs from the Ascendant sign, or from the sign of the Sun, or the Lot of Fortune (also known as the *Part* of Fortune), constituted the houses. In Chapter 3 on *aspects* you'll read that aspects were originally features of relationships between signs. Here you will learn how the zodiac was used as the basic reference for the condition and relationships of other chart factors. Then in Chapter 4 on significators you will read about *planets* and learn about putting together dignities, houses, and aspects to give information about a planet in a chart. In Chapter 5 on planetary sect we'll explore the differences between *daytime* and *nighttime* charts. In the Chapter 6, the final chapter, we'll examine the *planetary phenomena* of heliacal rising and setting, oriental and occidental positions, and reexamine the phases of the Moon.

What Astrology Gains by Exploring its Traditions

By the early 1900's mainstream astrology had taken much of its present form. Astrology had become simpler and more available to the general public but at the high price of losing much of the richness from the past. During this century astrologers responded to astrology's simplification in two important ways.

We expanded our technical scope, adding for example, symmetries (midpoints and planetary pictures), and harmonics. This work enabled astrology to use a more complex geometry. Alternatively, many of us went deeper into the mainstream astrology that remained, and its planets and elements and signs became psychological functions and collective archetypes. This allowed us to be more psychological and transpersonal in our astrological interpretations.

As we contact the astrology of the past, we also understand that traditional astrology too has always had its cultural assumptions and background. When we work with traditional astrology, we also work with many ideas at the root of Western culture, and we discover how similar and how different we are from our past.

One outcome from our study of traditional astrology is that we better understand astrology on its own terms. Instead of becoming more scientific, psychological, or spiritual, we allow astrology to be itself. To our modern mind astrology is one way we can contact the world's magic. As we understand our traditions better, we may find its roots in what we call "divination." Also, as we better understand how we use the visible sky for purposes of divination, the more we may find that this is not only the root of our profession, but also the trunk, branches, and leaves of astrology's historic tree.

The other outcome from our study is that we find a blend of traditional and modern astrological viewpoints and techniques that stay true to astrology's traditions, meet modern needs, and are internally consistent. This seems like a search for the Holy Grail and will probably take at least a generation to accomplish. Within that context our work in the late 1990's must be considered preliminary and probably quite naive. But also within that context is the excitement of exploring new horizons.

Unfortunately, astrologers frequently teach and write about astrology as if its current practices have always been part of its heritage. There are some surprising ways in which modern astrology differs from its past. I am not asking you to drop modern practices, but to consider them as recent developments and to approach them accordingly, *i.e.,* with curiosity and discernment. I am also not suggesting that you try to adopt traditional practices naively. We need to fully understand these practices exactly as they were applied, learn to apply them correctly ourselves, and then to rigorously test them for consistency.

○ Traditional natal delineation focused on *discrete areas of life.* Modern natal delineation often attempts to look at the chart as a whole and read it to get a glimpse into a person's essential being. Instead, traditional natal astrology works a birth chart one topic at a time. Often beginning with indications of vitality, length of life, and character, the astrologer gathers information about fame and fortune, relationships and marriage, friends and family. In horary astrology one will use only those indicators that are relevant to the issue at hand; traditional natal astrology works the same way.

In traditional astrology we do not see chart patterns as the bucket or the bowl, or aspect configurations like T-Squares, Grand Crosses, and Grand Trines. Nor did one total how many planets there were in fire or mutable signs, nor count voids in various categories.

○ Traditional natal astrology was much more concerned with *the world in which one lived* and *concrete situations within that world.* I'd like to illustrate this through the astrological houses. Commonly modern astrologers use houses to describe psychological tendencies toward the world, and many also liken houses to respective signs of the zodiac: houses themselves manifest certain kinds of energy. This is not the traditional use of astrological houses. Instead, the house of the father (the 4th House, by the way), was concretely about your father, not your father-projection, and the 2nd House was about your money, not your values. One may argue that this is a rather superficial way to go about doing astrology in our sophisticated times; I counter that this is where astrology can restore some of the world's magic.

○ Until this past century astrologers did not use *zodiacal* signs as intrinsic qualities or as personality types. When we, as modern astrologers, look at a natal chart for the first time, it's instinctual for us to look at the rough distribution of planets in various signs and especially the sign placements of the Sun, Moon, and Ascendant. When you read about traditional natal delineation, you'll find almost nothing about the zodiacal signs themselves.

From ancient times until fairly recently astrologers did not depict signs in a unified way but simply listed their qualities: Aries is tropical, cardinal, fire, bestial, of short ascension, ruling certain colors and items, and signifying certain features of weather and parts of the body.

How did astrologers consider an Aries Ascendant? The astrologer would notice that Aries is not a "human" but a "bestial" sign, and that as a cardinal sign there might be a more public display of oneself; more often, however, one would look directly for Mars, the domicile lord of Aries, as a significant planet for various issues in a person's life.

When, you may ask, did astrologers begin to use the elements of the signs for personality delineation or to depict one's "energy"? Except for using the sign of the Ascendant as one factor among others, it was not until the middle of the 20th Century that astrologers used elements in a psychological way.

o   Traditional astrology aligned itself more strongly with the *changing appearances of the surrounding* sky. Because mainstream modern astrology is based on zodiacal signs and planetary aspects, and because we do not make clear distinctions between planets that are visible and planets that are not visible, our experience of the astrological sky has become more purely mental. (Astrology's computer age has of course exacerbated this.) As one works with the astrology of our ancestors, however, one finds a new appreciation for the visible movements of the planets and the entire sky itself.

The Background of Traditional Astrology

It is most convenient to divide traditional astrology's literature into two major eras: the Hellenistic Greek era, and the Medieval era.

The extant literature of Hellenistic Greek astrology was contemporary with the Roman Empire but lasted until about 900. Its origins, however, were a few hundred years earlier, from the world of Alexander the Great. This astrology had its roots in Babylon but was strongly influenced late by Egyptian culture and by Greek philosophy. Its home remained throughout the Roman Empire, as long as there was a Roman Empire, and was most fertile in Egypt and the Middle East. Its language was primarily Greek as that was the language of culture and literacy at the time. Hellenistic Greek astrology resembles Jyotish, or Vedic astrology, although there are also significant differences.

Hellenistic Greek astrology arose later and separately from the Olympian religion of the Greeks, and flourished at a time when the Greek Olympian religion, with its Roman counterpart, had become mostly a ceremonial and political religion. Because our planets have the names of Roman Gods, and because Greek astrological writers call Jupiter "the star of Zeus" and so forth, it is natural for us to imagine that the Greek and Roman gods were prominent in ancient astrological understanding. This would be a great mistake; in its extant literature ancient astrology never tried to understand itself better through examining the Olympian religion. Instead, Hellenistic Greek astrology coexisted with many philosophical and religious systems from the Near East, out of which emerged the Christian religion. After the Roman Empire fell, Hellenistic Greek astrology survived in the Eastern world, especially within the Byzantine Empire.

After the rise of Islam and appearing about 900 C.E. perhaps from Persia, there appeared an astrology more like our own. The astrology emerging from the Arab world differed significantly from the Greek tradition, especially in its use of orbs for aspects and, more gradually, of quadrant house systems. This type of astrology came to Europe around the time of the Crusades, and was systematized in the work of Ibn Ezra (12th Century), Guido Bonatti (13th Century) and others. Over the centuries there were some developments, but in large part this tradition continued steadily through the Renaissance to the beginnings of the modern era. This tradition of astrology prevailed throughout Europe and its written language was primarily Medieval Latin. Although there were would-be reformers of astrology before William Lilly, notably Morinus and Johannes Kepler (all 17th Century), it wasn't until around 1700 that this long astrological tradition was seriously disrupted.

Now, without any further delay, we move to the astrology that we have inherited from the past. We'll look at zodiacal placement with disposi-tion and essential dignities, perhaps bring some new uncertainty about houses and aspects, combine all these into some interpretative work on planets as significators. Then we summarize two methodologies unused by most modern astrologers until recent times: planetary sect and phases of the planets with the Sun. May you have a good journey!

To my readers: (April 2007)

Ten years after finishing *A Practical Guide to Traditional Astrology*, I am delighted to present it once again.

This book continues to be a good introduction for modern astrologers to Hellenistic and Medieval techniques. Many astrologers now use the material in this book on their own. This is a good indication of its clarity and usefulness.

During the time I wrote most of *A Practical Guide*, I was involved with Project Hindsight, which translated many of the primary texts used to compose this book. I had the good fortune of hosting many workshops with Robert Hand on applications of traditional techniques for modern astrologers, At this time Rob was part of Project Hindsight, and translated many of the medieval texts. Robert Schmidt, who translated the Greek, helped bring out connections between the astrology and the philosophy of the day. He also helped elucidate the meaning of many difficult passages in the Hellenistic literature,

I also had the support of many newly minted traditional astrologers who are my friends and colleagues. I have found that indeed it takes a village to write a book.

Today it seems that many of the chart examples I use are dated: who now remembers losing candidates from the 1996 Presidential election or Andrew Cunanon? The astrology, however, holds up well. I have just a few conditions to attach.

Today I use whole sign houses exclusively in all my natal, horary, and electional work. In Chapter Two, when presenting whole sign houses, I stated that I wasn't fully convinced that they worked better than quadrant houses. Changing from quadrant to whole sign houses took me many years to accomplish.

Today, when I work with planets and their configurations with the Sun, I hold to a simple distinction. A planet is oriental when rising before the Sun to its opposition and occidental from the opposition to setting to the Sun. In Chapter Six, in sifting through the many ways that planets configure with the Sun, I presented the concepts "oriental" and "occidental" in a different manner., I referred to the first and third quadrants and to second and fourth quadrants, as "oriental" and "occidental" respectively.

With these few changes, I incorporate most of the material from this book into my astrological work, to the benefit of my students and clients. I am happy that others who I do not know can have this same opportunity.

Joseph Crane
Bristol, Rhode Island

Chapter 1: Traditional Planetary Dignity and Disposition

Dignity and Disposition

The ideas of dignity and disposition are closely related — both concern themselves with an ability to function in a worthy manner. Before it carried the connotation of stuffiness or arrogance, the word *dignity* meant worthy, honorable, and excellent in quality. If a planet inhabits a zodiacal sign in which that planet is favored, then that planet has dignity.

But first, Medieval and Renaissance astrologers made a convenient distinction between *essential* and *accidental* dignity. Essential dignity deals with a planet's position in the zodiac. For example, Venus has dignity in Pisces because Pisces is the exaltation of Venus; Mercury has dignity in Gemini because Gemini is a sign ruled by Mercury. Accidental dignity is a result of circumstances in a particular chart — a planet's house position, relationship with other planets in a birth chart, and other factors. Venus in the 1st House, or trine Jupiter, are examples of accidental dignities, which do not relate to a planet's sign, but enhance the power of the planet. In this chapter you will be reading about essential, rather than accidental, dignity.

Disposition describes the power a planet has over another place in a chart, such as the Ascendant or the Moon or Lot of Fortune or the planet itself. For example, Venus is dispositor for my Libra Ascendant, and Mars is dispositor for my Venus in Scorpio. The word *dispose,* however, once meant to "place (things) at proper distances apart and in proper positions with regard to each other, to place suitably, adjust; to place or arrange in a particular order."[1] Some dispositors, however, are better managers than others. If Venus is dispositor for a Libra 1st House but is in detriment in Aries or Scorpio, she may not be able to act effectively. If Venus is exalted in Pisces, however, she can be happily and confidently Venusian.

Domicile Rulers

In Hellenistic times the word for sign ruler was *oikodektor* — *oiko* from the word for house or dwelling, and *dektor,* which means "to take upon oneself," "to be responsible for." This implies a function of stewardship rather than domination. Therefore, what we habitually call "rulership" is inaccurate from a traditional point of view. The sign ruler, more accurately called *domicile ruler,* functions as a chief operations officer or prime minister rather than as a king or emperor.

According to the Greeks it is impossible for a planet to "rule" a sign. Because the circle of the zodiac is unchanging and the planets change constantly in their orbits, the ancients gave the zodiac greater authority. The planets, however, interact with our world of change, and without the planets the sky has little meaning for us. It is incorrect to say that "Mars rules Aries," because what changes cannot rule what does not change. Nor is it quite right to say that "Aries rules Mars." Instead, if you want to know how Aries is doing in a particular chart, you could look for the condition of its domicile ruler, Mars.

From the circle of signs come the domicile rulers, and these rulers structure the circle of the zodiac for us.[2] The lights — the Moon and the Sun — are the domicile rulers of Cancer and Leo, respectively. Why are Leo and Cancer given as signs of the Sun and Moon? Because,

Figure 1.1
Dignities in the Zodiac

in the northern hemisphere, there is the *most light* in the summer, the months of Cancer and Leo, when the Sun is at his northernmost point. Then moving one sign each opposite direction the next planet Mercury is given two signs — Gemini and Virgo. Again, moving one sign in each direction, Venus is given domicile rulership of Taurus and Libra. Following this scheme Mars is given Aries and Scorpio; then Jupiter, Pisces and Sagittarius. Finally, Saturn is given Capricorn and Aquarius, opposing the signs of the lights.

Next, notice how the planets affiliated with the signs are in relationship to the Moon and Sun. Taurus is in sextile to Cancer; Libra is in sextile to Leo. Both Taurus and Libra are affiliated with Venus. Therefore, the sextile aspect has a Venus (minor benefic) quality. From Cancer the square is to Aries; from Leo the square is to Scorpio. The square is of the nature of Mars. Using the same method one finds that trines are Jupiterian, and oppositions Saturnian. Traditional astrologers considered the opposition much more difficult than the square!

Within this scheme certain planets naturally oppose one another: the Sun opposes Saturn, the Moon opposes Saturn, Mercury opposes Jupiter, and Venus opposes Mars. (See Figure 1.1) From these basic planetary oppositions we find the planets in their signs of detriment — the Sun in Aquarius, the Moon in Capricorn, Venus in Scorpio, and Mars in Taurus. Their chief operating officers (domicile rulers) are antithetical to these planets themselves. This is like Newt Gingrich trying to run a yoga center or Madonna being elected mayor of your town. When placed in detriment, the planet and the steward of the sign it occupies have different agendas and, therefore, act in an uncoordinated fashion.

Planetary Sect Influence on Domicile Rulers

For a more complete sense of what domicile rulers are about, it is important to mention the concept of planetary sect. The two sects are diurnal and nocturnal, and a chart is considered either diurnal (the Sun above the horizon) or nocturnal (the Sun below the horizon). Zodiacal signs in the fire and air elements have diurnal qualities, and signs in the earth and water elements have nocturnal qualities. The planets themselves are considered to be either diurnal or nocturnal. The Sun, Jupiter, and Saturn are diurnal, and the Moon, Venus, and Mars are nocturnal. There is much more to say about planetary sect later in this book in Chapter 5. I also refer to Rob Hand who has lectured on planetary sect extensively and has published a monograph on sect called *Night and Day*.[3] This is an excellent short work on ancient astrological techniques and their application.

How does sect impact planetary dignity? In a translation by R. Schmidt, Hephaistio of Thebes (4th Century C.E.) quotes an important astrologer named Dorotheus of Sidon, who lived two centuries earlier. This verse may surprise the modern astrologer.

Of these therefore Aquarius is Kronos' preference,
Zeus is pleased in Sagittarius, Ares in Scorpio,
Cyprus brightens up in Taurus, Hermes gladdens
In the Maiden; one house there is for each light.[4]

Except for the Sun and Moon which have one sign each, the remaining planets have stewardship over one zodiacal sign that is masculine or diurnal, and one that is feminine or nocturnal. For example, Mercury has stewardship over a diurnal sign, Gemini, and a nocturnal sign, Virgo.

However, each of the starry planets (Mercury, Venus, Mars, Jupiter, Saturn) prefers one of its signs over the other. For example, Saturn prefers Aquarius, a diurnal sign, to Capricorn, a nocturnal sign. Why? Saturn himself is diurnal. For Saturn "the malefic," planetary sect is a *compensating* factor. Saturn needs the energy and the light of the day to moderate his cold and dry style. Saturn may also rule Capricorn, but this can feel like two lead weights instead of one. Saturn in Aquarius is lighter and more creative, but quite focused. I take this up again in Chapter 5.

Let's look at the other so-called malefic, Mars. Because Mars can stand some cooling and moistening, he is a nocturnal planet. Therefore, Mars prefers nocturnal Scorpio to diurnal Aries. In Scorpio Mars is less impulsive, less inclined to throw his energy around wastefully. The planetary sect issue for Mars and Saturn implies that for these planets to really work well in a chart requires a moderating of their basic energies. They are malefic not because of their basic nature, but because they tend toward extreme expressions of themselves.[5]

Why does Jupiter prefer Sagittarius to Pisces? Since he is naturally cheerful, Jupiter is a diurnal planet. In Pisces Jupiter enjoys himself but is perhaps a bit more subdued and modest.

It is Taurus over Libra for Venus, since Venus (called "Cyprus") is more nocturnally inclined. We will, however, experience Venus as warming or cooling, depending upon the situation and our own chart.

Why does "Hermes gladden in the Maiden?" According to the logic presented so far, Mercury is more nocturnal than diurnal. It is, however, natural for Mercury to be infinitely variable and eternally adaptable. Mercury is quieter and thinks more clearly in nocturnal Virgo than in diurnal Gemini.

Planetary Exaltation and Fall

An exalted planet has major clout without the heavy responsibility. A planet in its *exaltation* is like a planet being an honored guest or being entertained at a posh resort. An exalted planet does not have to run the resort but is well fed and has a lot of energy and confidence. A planet in the sign opposite its exaltation is in its fall and is therefore uncomfortable, like being at a party with people who don't particularly like you. Exaltations and falls help to determine a planet's great fortune or misfortune — its *dignity*.

The origins of the planetary designations for exaltations are mysterious and somewhat controversial. They may have once been a competing system of sign preferences for the planets. Ancient authorities talk about planets being exalted in certain degrees of certain signs, but the significance of these particular degrees does not show up in Western astrology. The word for exaltation is the Greek word *hypsoma*, related to the verb that means to elevate, to rise to a height. The opposite word, what we call the fall of a planet, is *tapeinoma*, whose verb means to lower or humble, or to be downcast or dejected.

Exaltations are a different breed from domicile rulership. Each planet gets only one sign of exaltation. Since there are only seven classical planets but twelve signs, five signs have no planetary exaltations in traditional astrology — Gemini, Leo, Scorpio, Sagittarius, and Aquarius.

Unlike domiciles exaltations do not follow a logical scheme for sign assignment. There is, however, an interesting pattern. For the diurnal planets (Sun, Jupiter, Saturn), each planet's exaltation is *trine* to that planet's domicile. For example, Jupiter's exaltation, Cancer, is trine to his domicile, Pisces. For the nocturnal planets (Moon, Venus, Mars) there is a *sextile* between exaltation and domicile. Venus is exalted in Pisces, which is in sextile to her domicile, Taurus.

The zodiacal sign of exaltation (for example, the Moon in Taurus) has less in common with the planet in terms of obvious similarity than the sign of domicile (the Moon in Cancer). The exaltations of the other planets are the Sun in Aries, Venus in Pisces, Mars in Capricorn, Jupiter in Cancer, and Saturn in Libra. They all provide friendly environs for their planet but they do not repeat their functions. Mercury, having to be different, has Virgo as both his domicile and exaltation.

Triplicities and Planetary Rulers

Today we recognize "triplicities" as zodiacal signs of the same element, although writers such as Ptolemy (2nd Century, C.E.) were careful for other reasons not to use the four elements when discussing signs. Vettius Valens, roughly contemporary with Ptolemy, is the first known writer to use elements with signs.

We can determine the triplicity rulers by combining the dignities of domicile and exaltation with considerations of planetary sect. (See Table of Planetary Dignities, page 10.) There are two major triplicity systems. One uses three planets — each triplicity assigned a day, a night, and a participating ruler. This system is linked with Dorotheus of Sidon and was used well into the Renaissance.

Another triplicity system, using only two planets, was used less extensively but prevailed during the time of William Lilly, and therefore is better known to us. This system dropped the participating triplicity ruler, instead using the day and night rulers only. I'll begin with the three-planet system.

To use triplicity rulers you must differentiate whether a chart is diurnal or nocturnal. Again, diurnal means that the Sun is above the horizon, while nocturnal means that the Sun is below the horizon. (This is the same consideration of diurnal/nocturnal that we use for planetary sect.)

We begin with our familiar fire signs — Aries, Leo, and Sagittarius. Since the *Sun* is the domicile ruler of Leo and the exaltation of Aries, and is the most diurnal planet, the Sun, then, is the triplicity ruler of all fire signs in a diurnal chart. Since *Jupiter* is also diurnal and is the domicile ruler of Sagittarius, Jupiter is triplicity ruler of all the fire signs in a nocturnal chart. Jupiter is less diurnal than the Sun, and has less dignity in these signs than the Sun. *Saturn,* the remaining diurnal planet, is the participating ruler for the fire triplicity. You may ask, "Why not Mars? Mars is the domicile ruler for Aries!" Yes, but Mars is considered a nocturnal planet and thus cannot be a triplicity ruler for a diurnal triplicity.

Working with the earth signs to find their triplicity rulers, we notice that the *Moon* is the exaltation ruler of Taurus and *Venus* is the domicile ruler of Taurus. We can't use Saturn, the domicile ruler of Capricorn, because Saturn is a diurnal planet and the earthy triplicity is nocturnal! We cannot use Mercury (with great dignity in Virgo), because we need him elsewhere. Because no planet is more nocturnal than the Moon, the Luminary of Night, in a nocturnal chart the Moon is the triplicity ruler; in a diurnal chart, the less nocturnal Venus is the diurnal ruler. For the earth triplicity *Mars* is the third ruler. Mars is the remaining nocturnal planet.

In the air signs — Gemini, Libra, and Aquarius — *Saturn* is the domicile ruler of Aquarius and the exaltation of Libra, and is also a diurnal planet. Thus, planets in air signs by day have Saturn as a triplicity ruler! (Would you not rather have your Saturn in an air sign?) Since *Mercury* is domicile ruler for Gemini, all planets in the air triplicity for those born at night have Mercury as their triplicity ruler. The participating planet for the air triplicity is *Jupiter* because he is the remaining diurnal planet. (Sun is a diurnal planet, but the ancients were careful not to over-use the Sun and Moon).

In the Dorothean system *Venus* is the triplicity ruler for the day for the water triplicity, and *Mars* is given the night. Ptolemy, however, assigns *Mars* as the triplicity ruler both day and night, for both diurnal and nocturnal charts. The participating triplicity ruler is the *Moon;* hence we have the three nocturnal planets.

Using Triplicities for Disposition

Here is a text attributed to Dorotheus of Sidon, an important astrologer from the Hellenistic world:

> I tell you that everything which is decided or indicated is from the lords of the triplicities, and as for everything of afflictions and distress which reaches the people of the world and the totality of men, the lords of the triplicities decide it. . .[6]

Use of the three-fold rulers has a long history and varied uses. For specific issues many astrologers from the Greek era used the triplicity rulers (of the Dorothean system) *instead* of domicile rulers! Let's find out how.

But first we have to place the three in sequence or order of priority. If you are born in the daytime, with the Sun above the horizon, the first planet in sequence or importance is the diurnal one. If you were born in the evening, you would start with the nighttime ruler and the daytime ruler would be secondary. In either case the participating triplicity ruler would be third in sequence or importance.

You would look at all of the triplicity rulers of a planet or a house for issues according to that house. For example, for matters pertaining to one's father, you might look at all three triplicity rulers for the Sun; for career, it might be the triplicity rulers of the 10th House. For issues pertaining to physical viability and health, you would look at the triplicity rulers of the Ascendant and/or the "luminary of sect" (the Sun if you were born in the daytime, the Moon if you were born at night). You would also look at the domicile rulers of the triplicity rulers, to see how the triplicity rulers in your chart were supported. If these planets are predominantly in "strong houses," aspected by benefics or in dignity, this would be a positive indication.

Three triplicity rulers were also used to divide three phases of a person's life. For example, I want to find out about relationships throughout my life. Since I was born at night, I would look at the night triplicity ruler of the 7th House sign of Aries, which is Jupiter. That's the first third of life. I would continue with Sun, which is the diurnal ruler of the fire signs. For the last part I would locate Saturn, the participating ruler for the fire triplicity, in my chart.

Thirdly, triplicity rulers were important in house delineation. The earliest source for this is from the Arab tradition, one named Alezdegoz cited by Bonatti. As mentioned in the introduction, Bonatti was an important compiler of the astrology that emerged from the Islamic world around the time of the Crusades.

In Bonatti's description of the houses, he refers to the doctrine of Alezdegoz.[7] Depending on the area of life you're concerned with, you would use different triplicity rulers.

For issues of the *4th House*, the first triplicity ruler is about the father, the second one about cities and lands, and third one about the ends of things and prisons. For issues of the *6th House*, the first triplicity ruler is about sickness and infirmity, the second one about servants, and the third one about the usefulness and value of these servants. For the *9th House*, long journeys is the first triplicity ruler, the second ruler is religion, and the third triplicity ruler is wisdom, dreams, and "the science of the stars." The *10th House* represents work and promotion through its first triplicity ruler, the "voice of command" through its second, and its durability through its third. The *11th House* is about "faith" and "trust" (remember "hopes and wishes"?): the first triplicity ruler represents faith itself, the second represents friends, and the third represents your friends' usefulness or value. The first triplicity ruler of the *12th House* is about enemies, the second about labors (hard labor I assume), and the third about beasts and flocks.

In the next chapter we'll discuss the changing meanings of houses in more detail.

Using Triplicity Rulers for a Planet's Dignity

Both the three-fold triplicity system and the two-fold triplicity system (remember, the twofold system is without the participating ruler) were used to assess planetary dignity. For our purposes here I'll follow the depiction of Ptolemy and Lilly, where planets in the watery triplicity have Mars, not Venus, as their triplicity ruler by day.

We now find that planetary dignity becomes more complicated than you first learned, and perhaps some of your planets have greater dignity in a traditional system.

For example: the Moon in Virgo in a nocturnal chart is in her own triplicity and so has some dignity; this is because the Moon is ruler for the earthy triplicity at night. Mars in Pisces, by day or night, is in his own triplicity and therefore has some dignity. As we'll see with our chart example, Saturn in Gemini in a day birth is a dignified Saturn. An essentially debilitated planet like Mars in Cancer or the Moon in Capricorn gathers some strength in a nocturnal chart through being in the sign of her own triplicity.

In some cases the strongest planet in a particular sign may be the one that is both exaltation and triplicity ruler. Saturn in Libra in a day chart is in his own exaltation and triplicity. The Moon in Taurus in a night chart is also in her own exaltation and triplicity. The Sun in Aries by day is also in his own exaltation and triplicity. After discussing the two remaining categories of dignity, we'll take up this subject once again.

Terms or Bounds, and Faces

Finally, there are other categories of dignity that have become important. However, they do not stake their claims over an entire zodiacal sign but instead over a portion of a sign. Terms or bounds divide all the signs into five uneven segments with each segment featuring one of the five starry planets. (See Table of Essential Dignities, p. 10.) A planet in its own bounds is enhanced. The first degrees of each sign, except for Cancer and Leo, are always the bounds of a planet that has some dignity in that sign. Bounds appear to give a positive or negative valence to a particular planet. A planet in the bounds of the two benefics, Jupiter and Venus, would have a positive charge, while a planet in the bounds of the two malefics, Saturn and Mars, would have

Table of Essential Dignities

Sg.	Domi.	Exalt.	Triplicities			The Bounds of the Planets According to Ptolemy					The Faces of the Planets			De.	Fa.
			D.	N.	P.						0-10	10-20	20-30		
♈	♂+	☉ 19°	☉	♃	♄̲	♃ 00-06°	♀ 06-14°	☿ 14-21°	♂ 21-26°	♄ 26-30°	♂	☉	♀	♀	♄
♉	♀-	☽ 03°	♀	☽	♂̲	♀ 00-08°	☿ 08-15°	♃ 15-22°	♄ 22-26°	♂ 26-30°	☿	☽	♄	♂	
♊	☿+	☊ 03°	♄	☿	♃̲	☿ 00-07°	♃ 07-14°	♀ 14-21°	♄ 21-25°	♂ 25-30°	♃	♂	☉	♃	
♋	☽-	♃ 15°	♀̲ ♂	♂	☽̲	♂ 00-06°	♃ 06-13°	☿ 13-20°	♀ 20-27°	♄ 27-30°	♀	☿	☽	♄	♂
♌	☉+		☉	♃	♄̲	♄ 00-06°	☿ 06-13°	♀ 13-19°	♃ 19-25°	♂ 25-30°	♄	♃	♂	♄	
♍	☿-	☿ 15°	♀	☽	♂̲	☿ 00-07°	♀ 07-13°	♃ 13-18°	♄ 18-24°	♂ 24-30°	☉	♀	☿	♃	♀
♎	♀+	♄ 21°	♄	☿	♃̲	♄ 00-06°	♀ 06-11°	♃ 11-19°	☿ 19-24°	♂ 24-30°	☽	♄	♃	♂	☉
♏	♂-		♀̲ ♂	♂	☽̲	♂ 00-06°	♃ 06-14°	♀ 14-21°	☿ 21-27°	♄ 27-30°	♂	☉	♀	♀	☽
♐	♃+	☋ 03°	☉	♃	♄̲	♃ 00-08°	♀ 08-14°	☿ 14-19°	♄ 19-25°	♂ 25-30°	☿	☽	♄	☿	
♑	♄-	♂ 28°	♀	☽	♂̲	♀ 00-06°	☿ 06-12°	♃ 12-19°	♂ 19-25°	♄ 25-30°	♃	♂	☉	☽	♃
♒	♄+		♄	☿	♃̲	♄ 00-06°	☿ 06-12°	♀ 12-20°	♃ 20-25°	♂ 25-30°	♀	☿	☽	☉	
♓	♃-	♀ 27°	♀̲ ♂	♂	☽̲	♀ 00-08°	♃ 08-14°	☿ 14-20°	♂ 20-26°	♄ 26-30°	♄	♃	♂	☿	☿
	+5	+4	+3			+2					+1			-5	-4

Underlined Triplicity Rulers are used in the Dorothean System only. Each Bound and Face begins at the degree plus any small fraction (*e.g.*, 10° 01') and ends on the exact degree (*e.g.*, 11° 00').

a negative charge. Using the table of dignities, notice that the last degrees of a planet are always the bounds of Mars or Saturn. Traditional astrologers also used bound rulers to predict length of life or for information on a person's body type.

Decanic faces seem more out of place in this multiple-dignity system. They do not relate at all to previous levels of dignity nor to diurnality or nocturnality. They do, however, follow a system of planetary days and hours, which was a mainstay of time-keeping throughout most of our history, and was a critical part of ancient and medieval astrological practice.

The order of the planetary hours follows the Chaldean Order of planets from slower to faster — Saturn, Jupiter, Mars, Sun, Venus, Mercury, Moon, and then Saturn again. Sunrise on Saturday is the day of Saturn and the hour of Saturn. The second portion is the hour of Jupiter, then the hour of Mars, then Sun, then Venus; and this succession of hours continues until sunrise the next day — Sunday, the day of the Sun, the hour of the Sun. Faces follow this same order. The first decanic face of Aries is Mars, the second is the Sun, the third is Venus; the first decanic face of Taurus is Mercury, the second the Moon, and so forth.

Looking at the Table of Essential Dignities on page 10, notice the first face of each sign. They proceed in the order of days! Mars is the first decanic face of Aries and is the planetary day-ruler of Tuesday; Mercury, the first decanic face of Taurus, corresponds to Wednesday; Jupiter, the first decanic face of Gemini corresponds to Thursday, and so forth.

Face rulers were used in Hellenistic Astrology but not as a principal dignity. Ptolemy doesn't mention these rulers at all, probably because their origins and rationale didn't fit well into his conceptualized system for astrology. Medieval Astrology contains descriptions of personality-types based upon the face ruler of one's Ascendant.

Peregrine Planets

What if a planet has no categories of dignity?

First I will illustrate what I mean by a planet being in no category of dignity. I will illustrate with another example from my chart. My Moon is 7 degrees of Sagittarius. Going to the dignity table the domicile ruler of the Moon is Jupiter; there is no exaltation ruler in Sagittarius; the triplicity ruler in my nighttime chart is also Jupiter; and the Moon is in the bounds of Jupiter, and the face of Mercury — hence, my Moon has no dignity where she is. In the medieval tradition this is called "peregrine." The good news is this: in natal astrology, peregrination was not the most important difficult factor; far more problematic would be a square from Saturn or being placed in a cadent house.

What could help a peregrine planet? There are a few possibilities, although the literature is scanty. The planet's next aspect might be to a planet that has dignity in the place of the peregrine planet. So that if my Moon applied next to Jupiter, this would dignify the planet; this is called *reception*. You will read more about reception in Chapter 3 on aspects. Another possibility, supplied in many computer programs that do essential dignity, occurs when the ruler of a dispositor is in the sign of the peregrine planet: to give a simple example, in my natal chart the Moon may be in Sagittarius but Jupiter is conversely in Cancer. This is what we moderns call "mutual reception," although this good news is compromised by the fact that in my case these two planets are not in aspect.

Although in later electional and horary astrology a peregrine planet can be a source of difficulty, I would not consider it a large debilitating factor in natal analysis.

Determining the Main Dispositor

The main dispositor is the planet in charge of the affairs of a planet or house. It is not necessarily the domicile ruler that has the most dignity in a sign! For the planet having the most dignity, which is often but not necessarily the domicile ruler, the Greeks used the word *oikodespotes.* The word sounds like "despot," and it does mean master or ruler of a house.

The planetary ruler, the *oikodespotes,* is the planet that has more authority than the other planets in a particular place in the zodiac. Consider the metaphor of a competition between planets to manage a chunk of the zodiac. Often the domicile ruler wins out, since it already has connections. But, because of the strength of exaltation and triplicity ruler or other dignities, some other planet gets the job instead. For example, a Midheaven of 9° Cancer is in the domicile of the Moon, the exaltation of Jupiter, the triplicity of Mars, the bounds of Jupiter, and the face of Venus. Although we would ordinarily look toward the Moon as ruler of the Midheaven, Jupiter — the exaltation and bound ruler — is stronger.

The Greeks would designate the planet with the greatest number of dignities as the planetary ruler, although, in other circumstances, they might use the triplicity ruler or bound ruler for a specific issue. Arab-era and subsequent astrologers numerically weighted these dignities unevenly, with domicile rulers getting five points, exaltation four points, triplicity three, bound two points, and face one point. With 9° Cancer at the Midheaven the Moon gets five points for being domicile ruler, Jupiter six points for being exaltation and bound ruler, Mars three points for being triplicity ruler, and Venus one point for the face. An Almuten is the planet who gets the most points of dignity for a particular place, and if the Almuten is in "good condition," this planet gets the job of dispositor. This word Almuten has been variously rendered 'lord', 'dominator', or 'victor'.

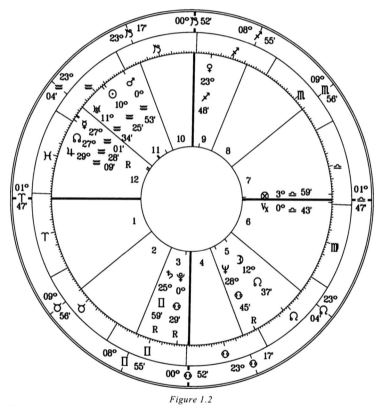

Figure 1.2

Thomas Merton
Jan. 31, 1915 9:00 AM GMT
Prads, France 44N13, 6E27

Source: birth records

13

Now let's apply some of these principles to Thomas Merton's chart, which is a diurnal chart. Thomas Merton was a renowned Trappist monk, essayist, poet, and contemplative thinker. He was an original thinker who loved rules and yet became increasingly nonconformist.

In looking at his chart, notice the mutual reception between Saturn in Gemini and Mercury in Aquarius. These planets are also in trine! This powerful and positive combination of Mercurial and Saturnine tendencies allowed Merton to articulate the merits of leading a disciplined lifestyle and of developing one's own vision and spiritual integrity. This combination also allowed him to be an effective communicator.

Saturn is also the domicile ruler of the Sun and the other planets in Aquarius. And Saturn in Gemini by day is in his own triplicity. Thus Saturn is the planetary dispositor and has his own dignity because he is in Gemini. (Jupiter in Aquarius, the planet associated with conventional religion, is in trine to his domicile ruler Saturn — he is "received by" Saturn.)

In Aquarius, as in the other signs without exalted planets (Gemini, Leo, Scorpio, and Sagittarius), the domicile ruler is also going to be the main dispositor of a planet. What the modern astrologer wouldn't notice is that because Saturn is the triplicity ruler of Gemini and is also in trine to these Aquarius planets, the trine becomes extremely potent and most beneficial.

Saturn has a great deal of authority by disposition. He "manages the affairs" of the 10th and 11th Houses, as well as the Lot of Fortune. (The Lot of Fortune, in Libra by day, has Saturn as its exaltation and triplicity ruler. Here is another example where the domicile ruler, which would be Venus, is not the planet that functions as dispositor. Merton was a monk!)

Merton stands out as a Saturnian person in a positive manifestation. He had a strong sense of values and purpose, and was a creative thinker. His sense of humor coexisted with an intolerance for self-deception. Merton saw discipline as the means to live most fully, not as a straight jacket.

Now let's take a look at Merton's three triplicity rulers and the thirds of his life. For him it is natural to look at the 9th House of religion. Sagittarius is the sign of the 9th House. As Merton was born during the day, his first triplicity ruler is the Sun, his second triplicity ruler is Jupiter (the nighttime ruler of Sagittarius), and his third triplicity ruler is Saturn (Sagittarius's participating triplicity ruler).

How is the Sun in Merton's chart? Although in fall and also peregrine, the Sun is in a strong house, the 11th, and is in close conjunction with Uranus. Merton was raised as a secular Protestant, became unhappy with the superficial nature of his young life, and went his own way to become a Catholic. In his early thirties Merton took monastic vows: this may correlate with a new triplicity ruler, Jupiter. The reader will quickly note that Jupiter is in the 12th House by Koch houses, which certainly implies reclusiveness. As we'll see in the next chapter, the Hellenistic tradition is to use houses based on sign, not quadrant. Nonetheless, Jupiter is favored by being conjunct the North Node and in trine to his dispositor Saturn. The third triplicity ruler, representing the final third of his religious life, is his all-important Saturn.

There are many other important features of Merton's chart, which I invite the reader to find. A classical astrologer would first look at the connections of planets and houses by dignity and by disposition and arrive at a dominant player in the native's personality. For Thomas Merton this planet is undeniably Saturn, with a major assist from Mercury.

These systems of dignities and disposition, developed very early in astrology's history, continue to be extremely powerful. If used appropriately, they can again be a centerpiece in the chart delineation of the future.

References and Notes

1. *Oxford English Dictionary*, *Vol. 4* (Oxford: Clarendon Press, 1989), 821-2.

2. For a discussion of domicile rulership, see R. Schmidt's trans., Ptolemy, *Tetrabiblos, Book I*, (Berkeley Springs, WV: Golden Hind Press, 1994).

3. Robert S. Hand, *Night & Day: Planetary Sect in Astrology*, (Berkeley Springs, WV: ARHAT, 1995).

4. Hephaistio of Thebes, *Apotelesmatics Book I*, R. Schmidt, trans., (Berkeley Springs, WV: Golden Hind Press, 1994), 30.

5. Ptolemy, *Tetrabiblos, Book I*, R. Schmidt, trans., (Ref 2 above)

6. Dorotheus of Sidon, *Carmen Astrologicum*, D. Pingree, trans., (Mansfield, England: Ascella Publications, 1993), 162.

7. Guido Bonatti, *Liber Astronomiae Part II*, R. Zoller, trans., (Berkeley Springs, WV: Golden Hind Press, 1994).

Chapter 2: Angles and Houses

Ancient and Modern Uses of Houses

How do we as modern astrologers use the twelve houses? In natal astrology the twelve houses describe different areas of a person's life — the 2nd House is the area of money and finances; the 10th, career; and the 11th, friendships. For example, a planet in the 7th House would function strongly within one's relationships, and the ruler of the 7th House would say something about one's relationships in general. In horary and electional astrology, which is concerned with events and outcomes, we use houses to find the planetary significator of an issue. For a question or event concerning one's children the planet that rules the 5th House (of children) becomes significant. Thus the astrological houses help bring astrology "down to earth" by providing for the details of life.

Modern natal astrologers note that planets in the 1st and 10th Houses act more strongly, especially when close to the Ascendant and Midheaven degrees. Modern horary and electional astrology look at house placement to tell how strong a planetary significator will be since the strength or weakness of a planetary significator may presage the success or failure of an endeavor.

In ancient astrology houses function in similar ways. They tell us about specific areas of life and about a planet's functioning. From the ancient astrologers we learn how our modern house meanings began, how they differ from our own, and how strength or weakness by houses was determined. The largest difference between modern and ancient houses is in the house system itself. But first we will examine some important terminology.

Our familiar word "house" is misleading. The Greek word *oikos* means house as in a dwelling. However, an *oikos* is not an astrological house but pertains to the sign ruler (domicile) of a particular sign — Leo is the house or *oikos* for the Sun, Cancer is the house for the Moon.[1] When we think of a person being in his own "house," we think of an environment that's familiar to him, where he feels at home.

The Greeks used a different word, *topos* (related to our word "topography"), for an astrological house, which simply means "place." A place is not necessarily a familiar environment.

The familiar word *horoscope,*(derived from the Greek *horoskopos* "the marker of the hour") was simply the Ascendant. Sometimes the Ascendant is just called the "hour." The Ascendant was used to locate oneself in time, around which one constructs one's place.

How do we find our place, our *topos?* We need a compass to set a reference point and a map to relate the reference point to a larger terrain. The reference point was the Ascendant where the moving sky meets the horizon in the east. The map was the sequence of the twelve zodiacal signs, or, as the Greeks called them, the twelve *zoidia.*

Whole-Sign Houses

When most of us saw our birth charts for the first time, we learned that the Ascendant was the 1st-House cusp, and the Midheaven, the 10th-House cusp. However, this quadrant formula for houses was not the customary practice of ancient astrology. Instead, the predominant house system of Hellenistic times was whole-sign houses. The entire sign of the Ascendant comprises the 1st House with the Ascendant falling anywhere as a degree within 30° of that house. For example, Figure 2.1 below shows the whole-sign chart of the conservative Senator and former presidential aspirant, Phil Gramm,[2] with his Ascendant falling at 28° Capricorn. With whole signs all of Capricorn and only Capricorn is his 1st House, all of Gemini becomes his 6th House, and all of Scorpio (including his Midheaven degree) becomes his 11th House.[3]

In a whole-sign house system lines between houses are very clear. Whole-sign houses are like the rooms of your house or apartment, each one with a boundary and a specific function; one conducts kitchen activities in the kitchen, living room activities in the living room, and so forth.

For readers with intercepted planets in your birth charts, intercepted signs do *not* appear in whole-sign charts — even if you were born in Anchorage! Interceptions occur when a sign is on a house cusp, the next sign is wholly within that house, and the next sign is on the following house's cusp. For some people their whole-sign charts are much clearer than their quadrant charts.

The sign of the Ascendant is the 1st House for the general issues of one's life. For specific issues or for other people in one's life one can use a planet or a Lot as a 1st House, and set the other zodiacal signs or *zoidia* in order from that house.[4] For example, if your Lot of Fortune is in Scorpio then Sagittarius becomes the 2nd House from the Lot of Fortune, Capricorn the 3rd House, etc. Using houses from the Lot of Fortune rather than from the Ascendant yields information about worldly prosperity or success. (We see an example below, from a delineation by Vettius Valens, 2nd Century C.E.) Other sources mention

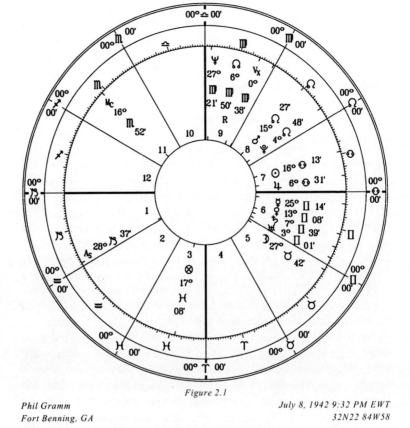

Figure 2.1

Phil Gramm
Fort Benning, GA

July 8, 1942 9:32 PM EWT
32N22 84W58

In this Whole-Sign chart, the entire sign of the Ascendant is in the 1st house, even if the Ascendant is 28°. Note that the Midheaven falls in the 11th house.

using houses from the Sun's sign (what we call "solar houses") to describe details about one's father.

Related to whole-sign houses was the fact that, for the Greeks, planets aspect one another, from sign to sign, regardless of orb. This is not different from how we practice astrology! Most of us would think about the Moon in Leo square Saturn in Scorpio in terms of the Moon square Saturn, Leo square Scorpio. You may then consider how the 6th House squares the 9th House. In ancient astrology planets that aspect each other are in signs and houses which also aspect each other in the

18

same manner. Astrology regains clarity.

Are whole-sign houses a quaint or simplistic feature of a primitive astrological method succeeded by our better technology? I think not. There seems to be a different, but not necessarily inferior, understanding of mind and reality. The Greeks looked upon signs (or *zoidia*) and degrees (or *moirai*, from the word which means fate) not as arbitrary standards of measurement to be subdivided for increasing levels of precision, but as basic principles of nature.

Houses as Indicators of Planetary Strength

To discuss planetary strength the Greeks used simple words from the business world. Houses, or places, that strengthen their inhabiting planets are "profitable places," *chrematistikoi topoi* which allow them to conduct their business well. Conversely, planets could be in unprofitable places where they "are shown to be ineffectual and inactive for the actualization of their effects."[5]

Interestingly, the word *chrematistikos* carries another meaning "oracular." With Greek astrological terminology one frequently finds interesting double-meanings. Here we could say "auspicious" as well as "profitable."

Where are the profitable places; where are the unprofitable places? There are two main criteria. The first is the familiar matter of angular, succedent, and cadent, and the second derives from the aspects that a house makes to the house of the Ascendant. "Profitable" and "unprofitable" places are environments that help or hinder a planet in its functioning. I may be the best hot dog vendor in the whole world, and if I get a franchise at Fenway Park in Boston, I will turn a great profit. However, if my place is in the Upper Yukon, I will not do so well. That is the fate of a dignified planet in an unprofitable place.

Note Phil Gramm's Mercury is dignified in Gemini (its sign ruler or domicile), but is in the 6th Sign or House, where it is considered "unprofitable." When he was young, Gramm flunked two grades in school! Compare that to his Sun and Jupiter in his "profitable" 7th Sign or House, which strengthens both the Sun and Jupiter.

A planet that rules a house or place has "dealings" or "does business" with that house or place. The word *chrematizo* which means "to have dealings" is from the Greek word for "money" and describes commercial transactions. Gramm's Jupiter in a strong angular 7th House "has dealings" with a difficult cadent 12th House. So far in his career Gramm has rebounded well from adversity, and it often seems that his difficulties have made him stronger. A planet's dispositor in a strong house can strengthen a planet in a difficult house.

A planet can be in an unprofitable place (like the 6th Sign or House) and do business in a profitable place (like the sign of the Ascendant); or, we would say, "the ruler of the 1st House is in the 6th." This *reverses the situation* in the previous paragraph. Now the ruler of a strong house is in a difficult house. A planet in an unprofitable place won't have much to offer to the 1st House. It is like an underweight person trying out for a football team or someone trying to buy a house without money for a down-payment.

Ancient astrology works with the ordinary commerce of this world. Planets with difficult house placements, or "place positioning," may be unable to run a profit in an ordinary sense but may be important for one's personal or spiritual evolution. Sometimes the 90 pound weakling becomes a spiritual Charles Atlas.

Pivots, Post-Ascensions, and Declines

Paramount in profitability is what we call angularity. Today we use the word cardinal for the signs Aries, Cancer, Libra, and Capricorn, but the ancients used "cardinal" for the angular houses — 1st, 4th, 7th, and 10th.[6] The word cardinal is from the Latin *cardo,* which refers to the hinge on a door (swinging one way, then another), and relates to our idea of "pivotal." The Greeks used the word *kentron* (also the source of the word *kendra* in Jyotish), which means sharp point but also "the stationary point of a pair of compasses, the centre of a circle."[7] Robert Schmidt translates angular houses as the "pivot points." (See Figure 2.2) Why was angularity so important to the Greeks? If, as Schmidt has suggested, astrological delineation was once analogous to formal ritual, setting the directions of east, south, west, and north is an important first step in both endeavors.

What we call the succedent houses, the 2nd, 5th, 8th, and 11th, are "post-ascending," and they have a neutral quality. Cadent houses, the 3rd, 6th, 9th, and 12th, are translated as "declines," *apoklima,* meaning a falling away but also declining or degenerating. (Our word "cadent," like the English word "cascade," has an archaic use as "falling.")[8] The cadent houses, without help from elsewhere, cannot provide an environment for planets which inhabit them to flourish.

A case example, delineated by Vettius Valens from late in the 2nd Century C.E., shows the importance of angularity. The topic of *Book II* of his *Anthology* is wealth, fortune, and happiness.[9] He discusses an

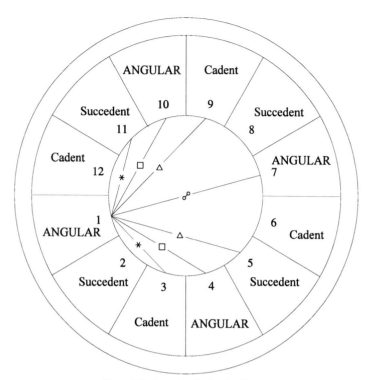

Figure 2.2: Assessing the Twelve Houses

individual who did well in spite of difficult beginnings. (See Figure 2.3)
Valens assesses happiness and prosperity by investigating the luminary
of sect (the Sun in a daytime chart, the Moon in a nighttime chart),
using that luminary's three Dorothean triplicity rulers. (I discussed
Dorothean triplicity rulers in some detail in Chapter 1.)

Since the Sun is above the horizon, this is a diurnal chart, and we look
to the Sun. The Sun is in Aquarius in the air triplicity, and has for triplicity
rulers Saturn (day), Mercury (night), and Jupiter (participating). Saturn
represents the first third of life and is in the 9th House, a cadent house.
Therefore, this person had a difficult beginning. The other
triplicity rulers, Mercury and Jupiter, are in the 7th and 4th Houses,
respectively — the houses of the angles from the Ascendant. Because the
Sun's other triplicity rulers, Mercury and Jupiter, are located in
profitable environments, the person will have better luck later in life.

Valens does not mention that the chart contains Saturn in fall in

Aries, the Moon in fall in Scorpio, and the Sun in fall in Aquarius. Essential dignity (the result of a planet's sign placeent) was less important than house position to indicate worldly happiness and prosperity.

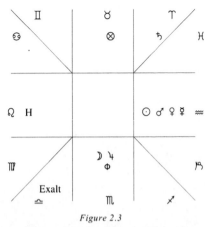

Figure 2.3

Like any good astrologer, Valens seeks corroborating testimony elsewhere in the chart. Valens sees the Lot of Fortune in Taurus and the Exaltation of the Nativity (another Part or Lot)[10] in Libra both of which are ruled by Venus. Venus has dealings with the zodiacal signs, or *zoidia,* that contain two important place markers. Where is Venus in this chart? "[We found] the lady (Venus) culminating with respect to the Lot [of Fortune] and elsewise upon a pivot point." Venus is not only in the 7th House — a profitable place — but the 10th House from the Lot of Fortune. The ruler of a Lot in a profitable house from the Lot can do great business for the Lot.

Aspects to the Ascending Sign

One also determines a house's profitability from its aspect relation to the zodiacal sign of the Ascendant or 1st House. (See Figure 2.2) In *Book III* of the *Tetrabiblos* Ptolemy (who is roughly contemporary with Valens) seeks the strongest places for *the apheta,* the planet that helps to determine life expectancy.[11] The 11th House is a worthy place because it naturally sextiles the house of the Ascendant. The 9th House is superior to the 8th, because the 9th House trines the house of the Ascendant but the 8th House is unconnected to the house of the Ascendant. Although the 9th House is cadent and the 8th succedent, the 9th House is therefore superior to the 8th.

Houses below the horizon also provide stronger or weaker environments. The 3rd House sextiles the Ascendant and is a decent place although cadent. The 5th House trines the Ascendant and is a very good place. And the 6th House which, like the 12th House, is cadent and unconnected by aspect to the Ascendant is a very difficult house. The 2nd House is an exception because it is the sign that follows the all important ascending sign.

When is a difficult house, however, not such a problem? Paulus from the 4th Century C.E. tells us that a planet placed in the 6th House is much stronger if a planet in the 10th House rules the 6th House.[12] This is because the 10th House naturally trines the 6th House. Look again at Phil Gramm's whole-sign chart. (See Figure 2.1) If Mercury were in the 10th House in Libra, he would help any planet in his 6th House because his 6th House is Gemini one of Mercury's ruling signs.

A planet in the 12th House is stronger if the 12th has a 10th-House planet as its ruler because the 12th House naturally sextiles the 10th. Planets in angular houses are productive in themselves, and bolster the houses they rule.

More on Whole-Sign Houses

Did ancient astrologers use house systems other than whole-sign houses? The answer is sometimes.

In *Book III* of *Tetrabiblos* Ptolemy appears to use an equal-house system to find the places strong enough to support *the apheta,* the planet that helps indicate life expectancy.[13] With equal houses the Ascendant is the 1st-House cusp, and each house is exactly 30° from the Ascendant. Since Phil Gramm's Ascendant is 28° Capricorn, all house cusps would be 28° of each sign.

In an equal-house system house cusps aspect the Ascendant *by degree* as well as by sign. However, the house cusp is not the boundary of a house but the degree of greatest power in a house. In Phil Gramm's chart the Moon and Neptune very closely trine the Ascendant degree. In equal houses his Moon would be the 5th-House cusp and Neptune the 9th-House cusp. Therefore, the Moon and Neptune would be power places in Gramm's chart.

Ptolemy and others who use equal houses say that a house begins 5° before the cusp.[14] Later astrologers will also often say that a house begins 5° before the cusp. For you, the modern astrologer, where does a house begin?

Vettius Valens, in *Book III* of *The Anthology,*[15] in his own section on life expectancy, gives us another possible house system — take the number of degrees between the Ascendant and Midheaven and split this number into equal thirds. In the order of the signs the first third (roughly the angular houses) would contain profitable degrees, the second third (roughly the succedent houses) mediocre degrees, and the last third (more cadent) would contain planets that are profitless and ineffectual.

This system, now called Porphyry, is the first known quadrant system where the Ascendant degree is the 1st-House cusp and the Midheaven degree the 10th-House cusp. (See Figure 2.4) Antiochus of Athens, roughly a contemporary with Ptolemy and Valens, also uses quadrants.[16] He correlates houses with ages of life, beginning with the Ascendant. (In the same section, Antiochus also mentions that a house begins 5° before its cusp.)

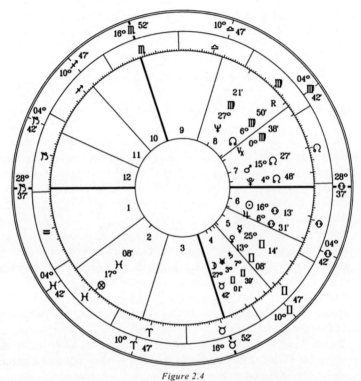

Figure 2.4

In this Porphyry chart this Ascendant is the 1st-house cusp, the Midheaven is the 10th-house cusp. All houses are 1/3 of the distance between the nearest two angles.

Other quadrant house systems from the Arabs to the present time build upon the Ascendant as the 1st-House cusp, and the Midheaven as the 10th-House cusp. (The Meridian system is a partial exception.) In order to find the intermediate houses many different ways have been developed. Some systems divide space by measuring from the equator or prime vertical; others divide the time it takes for positions to move through the sky. The Greeks had the sophistication to develop these other quadrant house systems but they did not do so. Their astrological orientation was primarily through the degree of the Ascendant and the circle of the zodiacal signs. Future astrologers abandoned the idea that houses are actually zodiacal signs and so used other means to derive the houses.

Shall We Try Whole-Sign Houses?

With the possible exception of the 4th-Century astrologer Firmicus Maternus[17] the Greek tradition used whole-sign houses to depict activities of life; they also used other systems but only to depict planetary power alone. Could we modern astrologers use both whole-sign and quadrant houses in different ways? Is it such a large jump to use quadrant systems to denote strength and the whole-sign houses for areas of life?

Many of us would blanch at an Ascendant being somewhere in the 1st House and not being the 1st-House cusp. Somehow that seems to be displacing the Ascendant. More troublesome, however, is the Midheaven degree falling in the 9th or, like Phil Gramm's, in the 11th House!

A Midheaven degree in a house different from the 10th is not such a calamity. We maintain our 20th-Century practice of using the Ascendant and Midheaven degrees for important aspects or midpoints. The Greeks, however, (who did not in fact use midpoints) would emphasize a midpoint or aspect that falls on the same *degree* as the Ascendant or Midheaven.

Rob Hand suggests using the Midheaven sign — regardless of which house this is — as a 1st-House marker pertaining to one's Midheaven issues, one's career or what one does.[18] The next sign is the 2nd House from the Midheaven sign, and so on. The relationship of one's father or family to career may be the 4th House from the Midheaven sign; one's business partner or agent may be the 7th House from the Midheaven sign.

For example, looking once again at Phil Gramm's whole-sign chart, the Midheaven degree is ruled by Mars, which is in close square to the Midheaven at 16° Scorpio. (See Figure 2.1) Mars is in the 10th House of the Midheaven further strengthening Mars. Gramm's Sun is in partile trine to the Midheaven degree, and in Cancer is in the 9th House from the Midheaven in Scorpio. Mars and the Sun are strongly configured with the Midheaven, as are the 9th and 10th Houses. We begin to see not only Gramm's personal ambition but his self-righteousness. Here we use the Midheaven degree not only as a sensitive point but as a 1st-House marker. This combines ancient and modern approaches.

The question for modern astrologers becomes: Should we attempt to use whole-sign houses? At least some of us should try them out. I have been encouraged but not overwhelmed by the results. Perhaps as I gain sophistication in ancient methods, whole-sign houses may become a powerful methodology for me.

To begin examining this system, you might look closely at your planets above the horizon that are in the same sign as the Ascendant. In the quadrant system these planets will be in the 12th House, but in the whole-sign system they are the 1st sign of the Ascendant. Are these planets more powerful, more part of you, than when in a weak 12th House? You may similarly look at planets that are in the 6th House but are in the 7th Sign from the Ascendant.

House Definitions: Ancient to Modern

From the time of the first Western contact with Arab sources in the 11th and 12th centuries,[19] our modern house definitions have hardly changed. Houses in Hellenistic astrology, however, show some different ideas.

Ancient astrologers used the sequence of the houses in the order of the clockwise diurnal cycle (reverse direction from the zodiac) to depict the ages of a lifetime. The main markers were, of course, the angular houses. The 1st House is the first period of life; the 10th (the Midheaven) the prime of life; the 7th (the Setting Place), one's old age; and the house of the I.C. (Subterraneous Pivot Point, the 4th), one's death and its aftermath. (See Figure 2.5) Modern prognosticative techniques, such as transits, secondary progressions, and the Huber system, go the other way counterclockwise in the direction of the zodiac.[20]

One feature common to both ancient and medieval sources is that certain planets delight in specific houses. I suspect that modern astrologers dropped house joys when Aries and Mars were connected to the 1st House, Taurus and Venus to the 2nd House, and so on. Perhaps we can give the old doctrine another look.

(The reader who is familiar with planetary sect will notice that the house joys of the diurnal planets — the Sun, Jupiter, and Saturn — are all above the horizon; the house joys of the nocturnal planets the Moon, Venus, Mars — are all below the horizon. Only Mercury is in between!)

1st House. This important house has changed the least over the years.

The 1st House concerns life, the energies for life, and the temperament and psychology of the native or querant. The Ascendant is also the first age of life because this is where the Sun rises in the morning to start the day. The Ascendant figures prominently for issues concerning the body: the physical vitality of the native and his or her length of life. Mercury rejoices in this house, not Mars (as moderns would have Mars and the 1st House affiliated with the sign Aries). Ancient authorities would consider it unbelievable that future astrologers could correlate the critical 1st House with a planet of extremes and destruction!

2nd House. This house is also about life, as having a living or livelihood. As this house (or *zoidion*) is naturally trine to the 10th House, it helps give vocational determinations. The 2nd House is called the *Gate of Hades* since, following the 1st House, the 2nd House is underground. Benefics (Venus, Jupiter) or malefics (Mars, Saturn) in the 2nd House help or hurt in acquiring property. Supporting the 1st House in a material way defines the 2nd House in both ancient and modern times.

3rd House. In both ancient and modern times this house is about siblings and neighbors or friends. The 3rd House is also the house of travelers because of its opposition to the 9th House. In ancient times the 3rd House was the *Good Decline* (cadent but sextile to the Ascendant) and the *House of the Moon Goddess*. The 3rd House connects to religious sects, especially feminine ones. According to Vettius Valens,

> And if the star of Hermes should be present together with the Moon in the *zoidion* of the Goddess and should have authority over the [Lot of] Fortune or the *Horoskopos*, the native will tell the future for everyone and will participate in the mysteries of the gods.[21]

The 3rd House may be of particular interest to those who follow unconventional religious paths, especially those with roots in Native American spirituality or paganism. These spiritual paths emphasize nature and the feminine. The Moon (not Mercury) rejoices in this house.

4th House. According to Firmicus, "This house shows us family property, substance, possessions household goods, anything that pertains to hidden and recovered wealth."[22] The 4th House is the place most underground.

The 4th House is also that of the father: the individual father, as well as the family lineage and inheritance passed through the father. (Generally the Sun and the Lot of the Father gave personal information about one's father.) Today we can use the 4th House for one's entire family inheritance — materially, culturally and emotionally.

In Greek astrology, the 4th House was also about the end of life and the aftermath of one's death. In traditional and modern horary, and event astrology, one can find the outcome of a matter from the 4th House and its ruler.

5th House. This is the house of *Good Fortune*, and Venus is in her joy here. All authorities, ancient and modern, use this house to describe children. In spite of this house being the joy of Venus, pleasures and sensual enjoyments were not emphasized until later. There is no mention anywhere of the 5th House and creativity.

6th House. This is the house of *Bad Fortune* dealing with illness, injury, and suffering. Because the 6th House does not classically aspect the 1st House, it is in aversion to the ascending sign. Illness undoes the vitality of the 1st House. The 6th House's affiliation with work is because of the trine to the 10th House. Because the 6th House is cadent, it brings not accomplishment but overwork (Al-Biruni)[23] or slavery (Paulus).[24]

In ancient times, the 6th House, not the 7th House, described enemies and contention. This is similar to the 6th House in Jyotish.[25] Phil Gramm has three classical planets (including a dignified Mercury in Gemini) in his 6th House. Like his friend Newt Gingrich, many dislike Gramm personally.

Mars is in his house joy in the 6th House. There are three possibilities for this: The cadency of the 6th House may weaken Mars into greater reasonableness; difficulties may bring out Mars's resiliency; or, following Hindu delineations, one can fight hard against one's enemies!

7th House. All authorities, ancient and modern, use the 7th House to denote marriage and marriage partners. Although powerful as an angular house, the 7th House can be a cause of difficulty, because it opposes the sign of the Ascendant. Because the 7th House is the *Setting Place*, as the Sun and planets set daily under the Descendant, this house is also about one's old age. Because the lights go out in the Setting Place, Paulus and Vettius Valens find significators for death more than for enemies. For Al-Biruni and Bonatti (and us modern people), the 7th House covers contentions and contests.

Jupiter in sect in the 7th House, according to Firmicus, indicates wealth and a happy old age. Since Phil Gramm was born at night, however, his Jupiter is out of sect. "For the native will lose a beloved wife and see the deaths of children. Late in life, however, he will receive an increase in income, not very large, but enough to keep him from want."[26] Jupiter provides modestly for one's old age.

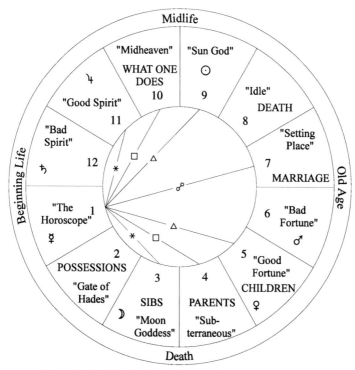

Figure 2.5: Defining the Twelve Houses in the Greek Astrology Era

8th House. Like the 6th House, the sign of the 8th House is not classically aspected by the Ascendant. It is in aversion to the 1st House, and hence called *Idle*. Indeed, death undoes the vitality of the 1st House, and all authorities use the 8th House as the signifier of death. The Moon does well in this house but only in a nocturnal birth (Firmicus), or when it is a waxing Moon (Paulus). The 8th House also signifies legacies which we find in Paulus,

> This place is established as dysfunctional, and when benefics happen to be upon this place, they make for profits from deaths; for they give inheritances, and they show those who profit from deadly motives.[27]

9th House. This is the house of the *Sun God* or at least of the sanctioned religion. According to Vettius Valens, if the ruler of the Lot of Fortune or the Ascendant is in the 9th House, "This child will be blessed, a prophet of the great god, and he will be listened to as a god."[28] Travel, then as now, is a 9th-House activity. Both Firmicus and Paulus affiliate the 9th House with dreams which continued into modern times. The Sun is in his joy here. (Note that the Moon is in her joy in the opposite house, the 3rd.)

10th House. This is the house of *praxis,* one's activity of life. The 10th House covers a wide area — work, reputation and profession, one's creative output, and, according to Ptolemy, one's children. The affairs of this house — planets within the house, the condition of the planet ruling the house — describe one's major activities of life and degree of success.

If one's beginning in life is the Ascendant and 1st House, and one's old age is the Descendant and 7th House, the 10th House is the middle years of life — perhaps our most productive time.

I do not find any Greek reference made to the 10th House being one's boss or, as Al-Biruni says, the rule of Sultan.[29] Thematically, the 10th House seems more like the Sun than Saturn.

11th House. This is the house of *Good Spirit* or *Good Divinity* and carries the usual definitions of friends and expectations, yet with a mundane significance of fame and fortune. This house contains a surprise, found in Vettius Valens,

> The 11th place from the Lot of Fortune is an acquisitive place, a bestower of belongings and goods, and especially when the benefics are upon it or are testifying.[30]

Since the 11th House is post-ascension of the 10th House and is in sextile to the Ascendant, I would think the 11th House a rather fortunate place. Rob Hand has commented that the 2nd is the money you have, and 11th is the money you make.[31] It will be no surprise that Jupiter rejoices in the 11th House, and all delineations of Jupiter in this house stress the native's eminence and glory. (Note that the house of Good Spirit, with its affiliation to Jupiter, is opposite the house of Good Fortune, with its affiliation to Venus.)

12th House. There's not much good found here from both ancient and subsequent authorities. The 12th is the Bad Spirit, and brings suffering and difficulty to the affairs of any planet in that house, with one exception. Saturn rejoices in the 12th House. "And it [Saturn completely in sect] will always make those who prevail over their enemies and oppress them, and those who are proudly confident in their own work."[32] When Saturn is completely in sect, the Sun and Saturn are above the horizon and Saturn appears in a masculine (fire or air triplicity) zodiacal sign.

Otherwise, it's bad news. According to Firmicus the 12th House determines enemies, slaves, defects, and illnesses. From medieval astrology we get the more specific idea of confinement. The 12th House, cadent, and not connected to the Ascendant, is a place of difficulty.

Postscript: Phil Gramm and his Planetary Periods

Since Mr. Gramm's presidential bid failed miserably in 1996, it is appropriate to look at indications using Hellenistic or Medieval predictive techniques. (See Figure 2.1) This is an opportunity to discuss the "chronocrator" or "time lord" systems of Alfridaries or Firdar, and Decennials.

Modern astrologers work their predictions by some measure of continual motion, *e.g.,* transits, secondary progressions, solar arc directions. Older techniques rely more upon planetary periods, similar in form to Dasas and Bukhtis in Jyotish. Different planets are assigned longer "major" periods and within them shorter times or "subperiods." According to the natures of the planets which have the times and how they are situated in a natal chart, the native meets the vicissitudes of life.

Alfridaries or Firdar, one of the simplest systems of this kind, is not in the Hellenistic tradition but was used by Medieval astrologers. One uses the planets in descending Chaldean order for both general and specific periods. If you were born at night you begin with the Moon, and if you were born during the day you begin with the Sun. Phil

Gramm, born at night, begins with the Moon, and then Saturn, Jupiter, Mars, Sun, Venus, and Mercury, and then you add a few years for the Dragon's Head and Tail. Each planet has a specific number of years for its major period: Saturn 11, Jupiter 12, Mars 7, Sun 10, Venus 8, Mercury 13, Moon 9, Dragon's Head 2 and Dragon's Tail 2. For the subperiods, the seven planets are divided into equal divisions that add up to a general period's number of years: since Mars is 7 years, each planet gets one year each. Since the Moon has 9 years, each planet gets one year, 3 months and 13 days.

At the age of 49 everybody born at night begins a Venus period. That sets the general tone. Venus has the advantage of being a benefic, but in Gramm's chart she is "with Saturn" and in a cadent house. Unfortunately for him, his run for president coincided with some difficult subperiods. Trouble began after he had become the main senatorial backer of Gingrich's "Contract with America" which tied his fortunes with Gingrich and the Contract. In December of 1994, the apex of the "Republican Revolution," he ended a Venus/Moon Firdar and began one of Venus/Saturn. This difficult time ended on February 2, 1996, and another happier one began with Venus/Jupiter. By the time the two benefics took over it was too late for him to recoup his presidential fortunes but not too late for him to get out of the race gracefully and get another term in the Senate.

Another important planetary period system is called Decennials. They were used sparingly during Hellenistic times but much more afterwards. Like Firdar, Decennials begin with the Moon if one is born at night, with the Sun if one is born during the day. Each general period, however, is of the same length, 10 years and 9 months or 129 months. The sub-periods are of varying lengths depending on the so-called "lesser years" of the planets. Within 10 years 9 months Saturn gets 30 months, Jupiter 12, Mars 15, Sun 19, Venus 8, Mercury 20, and Moon 25 (these numbers all add up to 129). We begin with the day or night Luminary, and go in the order in which the planets occur in the zodiac according to a person's birth chart.

Gramm's Decennials begin with the Moon, then Saturn, Venus, Mercury, then Jupiter in 1985. Note that Gramm's Jupiter's is angular and in exaltation. This Jupiter period coincides with his rise to national prominence. The last three specific periods within his Jupiter had, however, planets in the 6th House as sub-rulers. Venus was the "sublady" from the beginning of 1994 to the summer of that year; Venus being a benefic offset some of the difficulties from her placement in Gramm's chart. From August 1994 to April 1996 Gramm was in a

Jupiter/Mercury period. With Mercury in dignity and ruling the 9th House Gramm assumed his role as a politician driven by ideology, which made him popular in some banquet circles and gave him "ready money," but was not enough to grant him larger public appeal. In April 1996 after he pulled out of the presidential race, Gramm began a major Sun period. In his chart the Sun like Jupiter is angular but is not exalted. His political career, it seems, will be significant as a Senator but otherwise not spectacular.

References and Notes

1. *Companion to the Greek Track*, (Berkeley Springs, WV. Golden Hind Press, 1994).

2. Lois Rodden, *Data News, #53*: AA birth chart provided by Steven Prisolowski, from Kenneth March and Florence Scroggins.

3. Although the Ascendant's location defines the 1st house, the entire 1st house is called the Ascendant. Although the Midheaven does not always fall in the 10th house, the 10th house is nonetheless called the Midheaven. The same words are used for specific points (Ascendant, Midheaven) and for houses (1st, 10th).

4. In this century, the Hamburg school of Uranian Astrology used houses from different personal points to establish places for specific issues of life. See R. Brummund and U. Rudolf, *Handbooks of Techniques for the Hamburg School* English edition, Kohlrautz, trans., (Plantation, FL: Penelope Publications, 1992).

5. Paulus Alexandrinus, *Introductory Matters*, R. Schmidt trans., (Berkeley Springs,WV. Golden Hind Press, 1993), Ch 24.

6. David Pingree, in his translation of Dorotheus's *Carmen Astrologicum* (Ascella Press) uses the word cardine for places at angles to Ascendant sign.

7. Liddell-Scott, *Intermediate Greek Lexicon*, (Oxford University Press, 1972 ed.)

8. *American Heritage Dictionary*, (Boston: Houghton Mifflin, 1982).

9. Vettius Valens, *The Anthology, Book II*, 35.

10. The Lot of Exaltation is as follows:

Day   Lot = Asc. + 19° ♈ - ☉.
Night   Lot = Asc. + 3° ♉ - ☽.

11. Ptolemy, *Tetrabiblos, Book III*, Ashmand trans., (North Hollywood, CA: Symbols & Signs, 1976), Ch 12.

12. Paulus Alexandrinus, *Introductory Matters*, Ch 27.

13. Ptolemy, *Tetrabiblos, Book III*, Ch 12.

14. According to Rob Hand (1/27/96), the 5° criterion may be used by Ptolemy only for finding the *apheta*, and not to delineate houses. *Tetrabiblos, Book III*, is not clear on this point.

15. Vettius Valens, *The Anthology, Book III*, R. Schmidt trans., (Berkeley Springs, WV: Golden Hind Press, 1994), Ch 2.

16. Antiochus of Athens, *The Thesaurus*, R. Schmidt, trans., (Berkeley Springs, WV: Golden Hind Press, 1994), Ch 47.

17. Firmicus Maternus, *Mathesis,* Bram trans., 1975 edition available through Ascella Publications and Ballantrae Reprints. *Book II* explicitly describes equal houses, although following delineations pertain to whole-sign houses.

18. Personal communication, 1/8/96.

19. I use two sources here: 1) from the 11th century, the Arab astronomer and astrologer Al-Biruni, in *The Book of Instructions, Wright* trans., 1934, available from Ballantrae Reprints and Ascella Publications; and 2) Guido Bonatti from the 13th century, *Liber Astronomiae, Part II,* R. Zoller trans., (Berkeley Springs, WV: Golden Hind Press, 1994).

20. There is one modern system, that of Wolfgang Döbereiner which does direct from the Ascendant clockwise giving seven years for each Placidus house which would give something equivalent to the Greek system. [Ed.]

21. Vettius Valens, *The Anthology, Book II,* Ch 14.

22. Firmicus, *Mathesis, Book II,* 48.

23. Al-Biruni, *The Book of Instructions,* 275.

24. Paulus, *Introductory Matters,* Ch 24.

25. R. Dreyer, personal communication, 12/95.

26. Firmicus, *Mathesis, Book II,* 81

27. Paulus, *Introductory Matters,* Ch 24.

28. Vettius Valens, *The Anthology, Book II,* 12.

29. Al-Biruni, *Instructions,* 275.

30. Vettius Valens, *The Anthology, Book II,* Ch 21.

31. Lecture, R. Schmidt, July 1994.

32. Paulus, *Introductory Matters,* Ch 24.

Chapter 3: Aspects in Hellenistic and Medieval Astrology

Aspects and Modern Astrology

There is *no consensus* among modern astrologers about aspects. Different astrologers use aspects in completely different ways. The confusion over aspects is enough to baffle the newcomer and give comfort to the astrological skeptic.

Here are some examples. What is the difference, if any, between a square aspect between planets in signs that naturally square one another, and planets that are approximately 90° apart but in signs that naturally trine (the so-called "out-of-sign aspects")? Are squares "difficult" or do they simply imply energetic contact? Is it better to use an eighth harmonic aspect (semi-square or sesquiquadrate) which is close in "orb," or a trine in which the planets are 126° apart, not 120° therefore in a "six degree orb"? How does one work with harmonic charts whereby an aspect becomes the basis of a new set of relationships between planets and can provide us new interpretative material? How important is the planet that the Moon next aspects in your chart? These issues are critical for not only natal but predictive astrology. Transits, the predictive technique most favored by today's astrologers, are considerations of aspect.

The better we understand our evolving tradition, the better we can make sense of all of this. This also allows us to understand ourselves better as modern thinkers. We find that Hellenistic, Medieval, and Modern traditions have very different ideas about planetary relationships. We may also find that our ancestors have something to teach us about astrological technique and even about reality.

Traditional Use of Aspects

Traditionally aspects were seen to influence one planet at a time and give information about how that planet functions. Modern astrology, however, emphasizes the entire natal chart. We stress how often a certain aspect occurs or does not occur, and we also stress aspect configurations such as T-Squares or Mystic Rectangles.

Imagine that you, the traditional astrological consultant, want information about a client and his or her long-term relationships. You look to the ruler of the 7th House. How do you assess the condition of that planet? We know already that the planet's sign and house position are critical. Does that planet receive an aspect from a benefic (Venus,

Jupiter) or from a malefic (Mars, Saturn), and is that aspect helpful or hurtful? Because neither the Sun, Moon, nor Mercury are benefics or malefics, we're much less concerned with aspects from them.

Your client wants to know what kinds of career would be best. Following Ptolemy's method (given in the next chapter), you've found that Mercury governs his or her career, but you'd like to be more specific. You continue reading Ptolemy. You read that if Mercury is the planet responsible for one's career, one could be an accountant, a scientist, an astrologer or soothsayer. If Saturn testifies, however, "Persons then born will be engaged in temples for the purposes of divination, and for the sake of their fanaticism." If Jupiter bears witness, however, "They will be painters, orators, or pleaders in argument, and occupied with eminent personages."[1] The nature of the aspecting planets gives more information about one's professional possibilities.

Medieval era astrologers emphasized another possibility. A faster planet applying to a slower planet emphasizes a particular leaning for the planet or the chart itself. Although this thinking does occur in Hellenistic astrology, Medieval astrologers develop the idea much further.[2]

When discussing traditional doctrines of aspects, we must not treat conjunctions to the Sun as if they were like other conjunctions. According to these doctrines a planet within 8° of the Sun is considered combust or within 15° under the Sun's Beams and debilitated. This is a matter we'll take up later.

Whole Signs, Entire Degrees

I can state the main feature of the Hellenistic tradition of aspects in one simple statement: a sign to a sign, a degree to a degree. There is no such thing as our modern orb! Using Princess Diana's chart (July 1, 1961, 7:45 PM BST, Sandringham England, 52N50, 0E30),[3] Uranus (at 23° Leo) opposes both the Moon and Jupiter, although the Moon (25° Aquarius) is much closer in opposition than Jupiter (05° Aquarius). In Diana's chart the Moon is "with" Jupiter, although they are 20° apart. Venus at 24° Taurus is not in square relationship to Mars at 1° Virgo (our 7° orb) but in trine because the signs Taurus and Virgo trine. (See Figure 3.1). The ancient tradition had a simple response to our out-of-sign aspects: they are impossible!

Aspects in which both planets are in the same degree of the signs they occupy are very strong. Two planets, one at 00°59' and the other

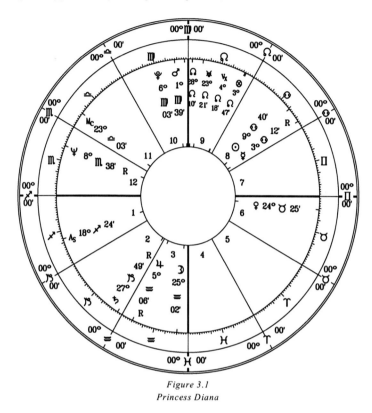

Figure 3.1
Princess Diana

one at 01°01' would not be within the same degree, as they occupy different degrees. Nowadays it is common among traditionalist astrologers to use the word "partile" to denote an aspect with both planets within the same degree of their respective signs.

We seem to look at lines of division as arbitrary and flexible like the lines that divide one town or state from another; when you drive the highway from Massachusetts to New Hampshire, you know you've crossed the state line when you see a "Welcome To" sign along the highway although the landscape seems identical on both sides of the sign. The ancients look at lines of division differently, more like those dividing the rooms of a house. Each room, then, has its natural integrity and function: you do not sleep in the bathroom or change your clothes in the kitchen. Similar are the houses and signs in a birth chart.

To the ancients a unit of measurement is not simply part of a language used among measurers but has its own objective reality.[4] This difference has profound consequences for the history of thought and science in the Western world. More immediately, it accounts for some basic changes in our astrological tradition. [These would include out-of-sign aspects, minor aspects like the semi-square, sesquiqudrate, and quintile, quadrant houses, and the modern theory of harmonics which is based on waves rather than on discrete units. Ed.]

In the last chapter we saw that **houses** derived much of their importance from aspects. The house in its aspect to the Ascendant tells much about a planet in that house. Because the 9th House always trines the 1st and the 3rd House always sextiles the 1st, both houses are positive places (especially the 9th) although both are cadent. We saw that we can derive houses not just from the Ascendant but also from Lots (*e.g.,* the Lot of Fortune) or Planets (in particular, the Sun and Moon), and that planets in signs angular to the sign of a Planet or Lot are critically important and could bode well or ill for the native. As moderns we frequently talk about angular houses and about squares being powerful and dynamic in a natal chart. This goes back to the days when squares and angularity were related closely to one another.

We also see how differently the Hellenistic and Modern traditions work with **transits.** To the Greeks, a "transit" was an *epembasis*, a "walking upon," which, in Latinized form, is the same as "ingress."[5] When a planet moves into a sign, whether it's Mars into Sagittarius or Neptune into Aquarius, it's as if the planet has walked into a room and has affected all the room's inhabitants until it has left the room. Whereas today we use categories of applying, exact, and separating when we work with transits, a Greek would look at a sign ingress and departure, and a degree ingress and departure. You can experiment with this yourself: does something shift or is there a relevant event when a transiting planet enters a new sign (and a new house for the native) and then enters the same degree aspecting an important natal position?[6]

The "Ptolemaic" Aspects

Often mentioned in one's introductory astrology textbooks or as part of one's astrological software, one finds aspects called "Ptolemaic." Ptolemaic aspects are the aspects of most of astrology's history; Ptolemy merely presented them. Today we consider as "Ptolemaic" the conjunction, sextile, trine, square, and opposition (no quincunxes or semi-sextiles, or semisquares and sesquiquadrates).

Ancient astrology uses different language for "bodily" conjunctions than for aspects. When planets are in the same sign they are "with" each other, but when planets are in signs that aspect one another they "testify," "witness," "scrutinize," "look ahead," or "hurl rays" to one another. When planets are in the same sign they seem to mix together; when they aspect, one planet perceives or gives testimony about the other. (Our word "aspect" means an appearance or view.)

The Geometry of the Circle

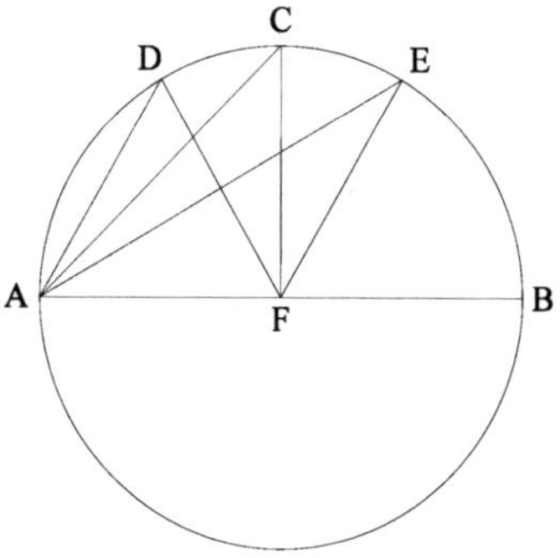

The next question is "why only the sextile, square, trine, and opposition"? In considering how easily modern astrology innovates, it's remarkable that the same set of aspects survived unchanged and unquestioned for centuries.

Ptolemy and others relate aspects to the geometry of the circle. The Hellenistic tradition uses aspect words that are geometrical: our opposition is their diameter, our trine is their triangle, our sextile is their hexagon. In *Tetrabiblos I*, Chapter 16[7] Ptolemy's description begins with the diameter which is a natural relationship because "it causes meetings on a straight line." Taking two right angles from that line, one has a square. Now go back to the original hemisphere and divide it into thirds, and one gets the sextile. Looking again on the whole circle, we find ourselves with divisions of two forming oppositions and squares, and divisions of three forming trines and sextiles. (See Figure 3.2)

Centuries later Ibn Ezra gives us a more elegant geometrical rationale.[8] Draw a circle from a central point C and divide the circle into halves at A and E by means of the diameter ACE

Figure 3.2

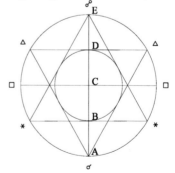

Figure 3.3

to form semicircles (corresponding to the opposition), then draw a line perpendicular to the original diameter through the center C to mark the squares. Make another line perpendicular at D $^3/_4$ of the way from the beginning of the diameter at A: the two points where this new perpendicular intersects the circle form an equilateral triangle to the original point. Place another perpendicular at B $^1/_4$ of the way up the diameter from A. Where this perpendicular meets the circle forms another equilateral triangle with the other end of the diameter at E. When you do this, the points on the circle mark hexagons (sextiles), squares, and triangles (trines) and the opposition.[9] (See Figure 3.3)

Here we find ourselves with another gap across the centuries. We moderns tend to view these shapes and symmetries as fascinating and entertaining to the mind. In ancient culture geometry was a sacred science and it is through geometrical pattern that nature and divinity divulge themselves to us. The Greeks would think us simpleminded for dividing the same number by two again and again to form aspects of 90, 45°, 22$^1/_2$°, 11$^1/_4$°. Nor were the Greeks interested in exponent progressions that form, for example, harmonics of 3, 9, 27 or 5, 25, 125. Although both Jyotish and Hellenistic astrology used harmonics, neither related them to aspects or aspect families.

Meanings of Aspects

According to Ptolemy and Paulus Alexandrinus trines and sextiles are harmonious because they are of planets in either masculine (modern fire and air) or feminine (modern earth and water) signs. Squares between planets that are also in signs that are in square will place one planet in a masculine sign against one in a feminine. Oppositions, however, are between signs both of which are either masculine or feminine but, by being on opposite sides of a circle, an opposition pits planets in otherwise compatible signs against each other.

When in Chapter 1 we discussed the domiciles of the planets, we found a pattern that shows harmonious and difficult aspects. (See Chapter 1, page 2) In a circle with Cancer and Leo on the top see the relationships between the signs of the domiciles of the benefics and malefics.[10] For sextiles, cast Cancer backwards to Taurus and Leo forward to Libra. As Taurus and Libra are the domiciles of Venus, sextiles are of the nature of Venus. Because Venus is the "lesser benefic," sextiles are good and pleasant. If, then, Cancer squares Aries and Leo squares Scorpio, both signs being the domiciles of Mars, squares are of the nature of Mars: difficult, stressful, disagreeable. Since from Cancer one goes backwards to trine Pisces and from Leo forward to Sagittarius, trines are therefore of the nature of the greater benefic Jupiter. Trines offer abundance, opportunity, and good fortune. Because the signs of Saturn (Capricorn, Aquarius) oppose those of the Lights (Cancer, Leo), oppositions are Saturnine, and represent blockage, oppression, and decay. (Traditional astrology finds oppositions more difficult than squares; we think of squares as a more difficult aspect than oppositions.)

This formula does not use semi-sextiles which would relate Cancer to Gemini and Leo to Virgo, both domiciles of Mercury. Because Mercury is neither a benefic nor a malefic, he does not fall into the same categories as the other four planets. According to ancient astrology Mercury becomes a benefic when witnessed by a benefic, a malefic when witnessed by a malefic.

Ptolemy's view of the harmonious and inharmonious aspects, which we take for granted, was not uniform in Hellenistic astrology. As usual, Ptolemy presented a doctrine in a systematic form and later generations used Ptolemy as authoritative.

For Vettius Valens, an important contemporary of Ptolemy, the aspecting planet's nature as a benefic or malefic was more important than the aspect itself. A trine from Mars or Saturn could create problems for a significator. It would be better if these planets were in signs of aversion and did not aspect a significator at all.

None of the Above — the Aversions

Many modern astrologers use quincunxes (150° or five signs apart) to denote aspects of frustration or irritation. Signs that quincunx, like Aquarius and Virgo, or Sagittarius and Cancer, are alike in neither quality nor gender, neither element or mode. Although signs in semi-sextile (signs next to one another) have the same features as quincunxes, modern astrologers do far less with them. Therefore, we should call both quincunxes and semisextiles "inconjunct," as they are not really aspects at all from the ancient perspective.

According to ancient astrology two planets in signs that do not connect by mode or gender are averse to each other: aversion not an aspect but a "falling amiss." If the Greek words for aspects are all words for seeing and perceiving, signs that are averse do not "see" each other; they turn away from each other. Ptolemy calls them "unconnected" and "alienated." This need not be a problem; if you're assessing Mercury, Jupiter in an averse sign may not help but Saturn in an averse sign does no harm.

A serious problem occurs if the lord of a house is in a sign in aversion to the house that the planet rules. In Princess Diana's chart the 7th House of marriage is the sign Gemini that has as its ruler Mercury, the "star of Hermes." If you look at Diana's Mercury, however, you find him in Cancer in the 8th House. Mercury in Cancer is in a sign averse to Gemini so that the 7th House and its lord cannot see each other. When there's an emergency, nobody can find the boss.

Cancer, the sign of Diana's Mercury, is the 8th House Sign of any chart with a Sagittarius Ascendant. Because the 8th House is in aversion to the 1st House, it's not a helpful place to the native. Because Mercury, lord of Diana's 7th, is in aversion to the 7th House and also to the Ascendant, marriage is doubly difficult.

One finds similar problems with Princess Diana's Lot of Fortune, representing wealth, health, and the changing fortunes of life. Fortuna itself is in a decent house (the 9th), the benefics are angular and the malefics are in aversion — great! The lord of Diana's Lot of Fortune in Leo is the Sun. Fortuna's lord the Sun, however, is in aversion to the sign of Fortuna and is also in the 8th House. Although on the surface Diana seemed luckier than most of us, her life contained great personal and public difficulty. Because the ruler of Fortuna is involved, her charmed life often had an unfocused and rudderless quality.

Here's an exercise you can do with your own chart. Use a whole-sign format and find the domicile ruler for each house in your natal chart. Does the ruler of a house connect to the house itself? Or is it in the 2nd, 6th, 8th, or 12th sign from the house it rules? Secondly, look at the angular signs and seek important placements in your chart like the Ascendant, Sun, Moon, Fortuna — are their sign rulers connected or unconnected? Furthermore, see whether benefics and malefics connect or do not connect with Ascendant, Sun, Moon, Fortuna by whole sign. Doing all this, do any patterns emerge regarding any particular issues in your life?

Exceptions to Signs in Aversion

Working with Hellenistic and Medieval astrology, we frequently read about techniques that we don't see in use. Paulus, Ptolemy, Hephaistio, and Firmicus Maternus all discuss signs in aversion that nonetheless have familiarity with one another. Firmicus gives us one rather strange example, using signs in antiscion relationship.[11] (Valens, who gives us many chart examples, neither mentions nor uses this material.) Because the tradition discusses these exceptions, I need to discuss them here.

One familiarity between signs is when they *share the same ruler.* Neither Aries and Scorpio nor Taurus and Libra form Ptolemaic aspects with one another, but Aries and Scorpio have Mars as ruler, Taurus and Venus have Venus. The other averse pair that share the same ruler is Capricorn and Aquarius both of which are Saturn's signs.

The next exception relates to *antiscia or having equal light.* Antiscia are points symmetrical to the solstice points 0° Cancer and 0° Capricorn, and relate to the length of the time during which a degree of the zodiac is above or below the horizon. In the Northern hemisphere 0° Cancer, the northernmost point of the zodiac, is above the horizon for the greatest amount of time each day; 0° Capricorn is above the horizon the least amount of time. This reverses in the Southern Hemisphere, where 0° Capricorn is above the Earth for the longest time. In either hemisphere 1° Gemini and 29° Cancer are 29 degrees from 0° Cancer and 151 from 0° Capricorn. They have equal light, that is, they spend the same amount of time above (or below) the horizon. The signs that have equal light are Gemini and Cancer, Taurus and Leo, Aries and Virgo, Pisces and Libra, Aquarius and Scorpio, Capricorn and Sagittarus. Signs normally in semi-sextile or quincunx — Gemini/Cancer, Aries/Virgo, Pisces/Libra, and Capricorn/Sagittarius — now have at least a nodding acquaintance with one another.

The third exception relates to ascensional times, or *signs of equal rising time.* Most modern astrologers know about signs of short ascension and long ascension. If you progress the Ascendant, for example, you find that in the Northern Hemisphere Aries and Pisces move rather quickly, Virgo and Libra much more slowly. That's because in the Northern Hemisphere the Ascendant rises most quickly near 0° Aries, most slowly near 0° Libra. How quickly or how slowly do these signs rise? Ascensional times between signs of short and long ascension are most similar at the Equator and most extreme near the Poles. The equally rising signs are Aries and Pisces, Taurus and Aquarius, Gemini and Capricorn, Cancer and Sagittarius, Leo and Scorpio, Virgo and Libra. Thus Aries/Pisces, Gemini/Capricorn, Cancer/Sagittarius, and Virgo/Libra are no longer averse to one another. These relationships, by degrees rather than signs, we call contra-antiscia.[12]

To return to Princess Diana's chart, the 7th House and its lord come together as Gemini and Cancer are of signs *equal light.* The 7th House ruler Mercury and the Ascendant also come together, because Cancer and Sagittarius are both *equally rising.* I leave it to the reader to judge whether these nullifications of aversion were sufficient for Princess Diana.

"Looking Ahead" and "Hurling Rays"

Now we come to one of most baffling features of ancient astrology, the doctrine on planets aspecting forwards and backwards in the zodiac. A planet can have a different effect from one side of an aspect than from the other side. There is not a mixing of energies between aspecting planets, as in modern astrology, but a dialectical relationship between two planets that aspect one another.

Take another look at Princess Diana's natal chart. There's a trine between Saturn in Capricorn and Venus in Taurus. Saturn makes his daily course through the sky before Venus. Saturn is on the left making an aspect to Venus forward in the signs; Venus is on the right making an aspect to Saturn backwards in the order of the signs. Future astrologers would call Saturn's aspect to Venus "sinister" and Venus's aspect to Saturn "dexter."

Antiochus of Athens, writing from the 2nd Century C.E., makes an interesting distinction: forward "sinister" aspects "look ahead" or "bear witness" to the succeeding star; the succeeding star "hurls its rays" back at the preceding star. In Princess Diana's chart Saturn "looks ahead "at Venus, and Venus "hurls rays" back at Saturn. The planet (A) which "looks ahead" to a planet (B) further along in the zodiac, and (A) which rises earlier in the day may carry the initiative to a following planet (B) ("following" in the order of risings) who "hurls its rays" back to the first (A).

One aspect relationship prominent in the Hellenistic Greek tradition is that of "superiority." If a planet is in a square to another planet so that one planet is in the 10th Sign from the other, a "10th House square," the planet in the 10th Sign dominates the other one. In Diana's chart both the Moon and Jupiter in Aquarius have "superior" position over Venus in Taurus, which would strengthen Venus as Jupiter is a benefic.

According to Hellenistic ideas on vision when we look at some-thing, the eye casts a ray which gives the object its form; the object perceived provides a second ray which provides the material principle. Remember that the Hellenistic words for aspect are about seeing, regarding, scrutinizing, and testifying.[13]

In a court of law someone can give positive or negative testimony about you, or you can be "scrutinized" in a withering cross-examination.

44

This can affect the outcome of the "trial" — the condition of a planet — in a positive or a negative way. How do you behave when, in a trial, you hear flattering or demeaning accounts of yourself?[14] You look back, and if it's negative testimony, you might "hurl rays" back to the witness. This is very different from our tendency to view aspecting planets as merged with one another, and one does not find these courtroom battles depicted in the Medieval or Modern astrological traditions.

Because the Hellenistic tradition uses aspects by sign, it's possible for many planets to aspect one planet and give conflicting testimony about that planet. One way to sort out "conflicting testimony" may be to give precedence to the planet looking ahead in the zodiac to the planet in question. In Diana's chart the trine is from Saturn to Venus more than Venus to Saturn. Valens, interested in Saturn's status as the greater malefic, has a rather unhappy portrait of this aspect; the square, however, is "much worse."[15] Firmicus Maternus is more positive as long as both planets are in a favorable positions.

Medieval astrologers frequently mentioned "dexter" and "sinister" aspects but did not appear to place much importance upon them; to modern astrologers they are just trivia.

Other Ways of Aspecting

Many modern astrologers use non-ecliptic contacts such as parallels and contra-parallels of declination and conjunctions of celestial latitude. These are not used, to my knowledge, before the Modern Era.[16] Although there was some use of ecliptic latitude to describe a planet, they made no use of it to depict contacts between planets. It's plausible, however, that parallels and contra-parallels of declination derive from the antiscion relationship.

Some ancient astrologers distinguished between aspects based upon distance in the zodiacal and based upon ascensional times. This is important because ascensional times were prominent in primary directions ("circumambulations") and for determining length of life.

Ascensional times count how many degrees and minutes of Right Ascension pass the M.C. as a certain number of degrees and minutes rise on the Ascendant. Degrees of Right Ascension measure along the celestial equator and relate closely with the diurnal cycle.

I was born at the 43rd parallel of North latitude in Boston, MA. I was born with Libra rising, a sign of long ascension; thus when all 30° of Libra rise, 38°26' of Right Ascension go past the Midheaven. A sextile between the first degree of Libra and the first degree of Sagittarius is just over 77° of ascensional times. An aspect that's a square between signs of short ascension (Capricorn and Aries) could be a sextile using ascensional times. Conversely, a square between signs of long ascension (Cancer and Libra) could be a trine using ascensional times. Later in the tradition William Lilly considered this factor and even used it in a horary example.[17] Although computing ascensional times is tedious to the modern astrologer, the computation poses no difficulty for the ancient tradition.

From the Hellenistic to the Medieval Era

When we move into the Medieval era, different thinking is at work and we find new ideas about aspects. This astrological style, the immediate predecessor of our own, contains more recognizable features. Medieval astrologers also present their astrology in a more uniform and systematic way, which is soothing to the modern mind.

Aspects carry the same function in Medieval astrology as in Hellenistic astrology. In natal, horary, and electional astrology, an aspecting planet strengthens or weakens a planet of concern, a "significator." A planet aspecting a significator modifies that planet according to the beholding planet's essential nature. Only in modern times do we survey all aspects between all planets.

Medieval astrologers begin to sort out the relationships between "good" and "bad" planets and "good" and "bad" aspects. (Nowadays we call them "easy" and "difficult.") Mars or Saturn aspecting by trine or sextile causes less difficulty than when aspecting by square or opposition. (Malefics also cause less difficulty in their signs of dignity than when in signs of debility.) A trine or sextile from Venus or Jupiter is wonderful, but that planet's beneficence decreases 1) if it is in square or opposition to a planet of concern, 2) if it is in a sign of debility, or 3) if it is in a cadent house, especially the 6th or 12th.[18]

We now explore Medieval innovations pertaining to orb, applying and separating aspects, and reception. These features, interesting but not significant to Hellenistic astrologers, assume great importance in the Medieval tradition.

Orbs of Planets, Orbs of Aspects

Today we use the word "orb" to denote how far apart two planets are from an exact aspect, and to note the maximum distance from exactness needed for two planets to have a particular aspect. The closer two planets are in orb, the stronger the contact between them. Different astrologers have different preferences for orb, and an astrology computer program that does not let you pick size of orb fails in today's market.

"Orb," as a word, is one of the peculiarities of today's astrological vocabulary. Your standard dictionary defines "orb" as a sphere or globe. "Orb" has the same word root as the word "orbit." Originally orbs were not about aspects but were spheres of planetary influence. According to Al-Biruni of the 11th Century the Sun has an orb of 15°, the Moon 12°, Mercury and Venus 7°, Mars 8°, Jupiter and Saturn have 9°.[19] Other sources cite slightly different numbers. Each planet has around it a sphere of light of a particular size, and the size of their orbs depends on how much light these bodies give off. When two planets are sufficiently close enough to each other, bodily or by "aspect ray," they behold each other within the "moiety of their orbs," *i.e.,* each planet contributes half of its orb to the aspect. Astrologers call these aspects "platic," unlike "partile" aspects which connect to the degree.

What, then, is the orb of aspect between Saturn and Venus? Saturn has nine degrees, Venus has seven. They combine to sixteen, and half of that is eight. Therefore, regardless of aspect, Saturn and Venus only behold one another within eight degrees. An orb between the Sun and Mars, however, is eleven and a half. This may be a "bodily conjunction" or "aspect ray." (See Figure 3.4 for a table of planetary aspects.)

Figure 3.4: Al-biruni and the Orbs of the Planets

	☉	☽	☿	♀	♂	♃	♄
☉	15.0	13.5	11.0	11.0	11.5	12.0	12.0
☽	12.0	—	9.5	9.5	10.0	10.5	10.5
☿	7.0	9.5	—	7.0	7.5	8.0	8.0
♀	7.0	9.5	7.0	—	7.5	8.0	8.0
♂	8.0	10	7.5	7.5	—	8.5	8.5
♃	9.0	10.5	8.0	8.0	8.5	—	9.0
♄	9.0	10.5	8.0	8.0	8.5	0.0	—

The planetary orbs appear to be based upon a planet's "arc of vision," and may relate to "combustion." "Arc of vision" denotes how many degrees away from the Sun a planet needs to be for the planet to become visible to the eye. "Combustion," given as eight degrees, occurs when a planet is so close to the Sun that the Sun scorches or burns up the planet's influence. The Sun's fifteen degrees is the minimum distance of any planet from the Sun's Beams. The Moon does become visible when she is about twelve degrees away from the Sun. The starry planets all have orbs that are close to the eight-degree limit of Combustion.

How do you determine a planet's aspects to the Ascendant, Midheaven, or Lot of Fortune? Because these sensitive points are not planets, they cannot have orb! In traditional temperament analysis one uses an aspect to the Ascendant only when the aspect is partile. Otherwise an aspecting planet's "moiety" can contact a personal sensitive point so that if Saturn's orb is nine degrees, Saturn could aspect the Ascendant, Midheaven, or Fortuna by four and a half degrees. Because they are not visible and so cannot have an orb, I would include within this category asteroids and the modern planets, Uranus, Neptune, and Pluto. To find the maximum allowable distance for an aspect of a classical planet from an invisible planet or to a personal sensitive point, use half the orb of the classical planet.

Joining and Separating

The factors of applying and separating are part of today's astrology, and are standard for horary and electional astrologers. Medieval astrologers also used these factors in natal astrology. From the ancients a different and more dynamic image of the natal chart emerges.[20] We become fascinated by the flow of time and how planets in a chart move over time.

A faster planet separates from a slower one, and when the faster planet is within orb of the next planet it *joins* that planet until the aspect perfects, then the faster planet separates from the slower planet until it joins the next planet.[21] The Moon often joins and separates many times a day.

The Medieval tradition talks about any aspect as a "beholding" but a planet's next aspect as a "joining." An interesting correspondence emerges. Remember that in the Hellenistic tradition a planet in the same sign as another one is "with" that planet. When a planet is in an aspecting sign it "scrutinizes" or "looks ahead" at the other planet.

In horary and electional astrology a separating aspect between significators pertains to past events and an applying aspect tells us about an outcome. Throughout the Medieval tradition the next planet any planet aspects is more important than any other aspect that planet

48

makes.

If you're looking for how the native will get along with parents, partner, authority, or royalty, and if the planet signifying that issue is joining the lord of the Ascendant, or the lord of the Ascendant joins that particular planet, this shows a harmonious relationship. (If the joining is by trine the relationship is better, and if there's reception it's spectacular!) If you want to find the "Significator of Manners" and there is no planet in the 1st House, you go to a planet that both the Moon and Mercury apply to, if there is one. If not, you next look for any kind of aspect to the Moon or Mercury.[22]

Look at your natal Moon and see which classical planet the Moon next aspects. According to eight hundred years of astrological tradition, this is a very significant planet. Note in Princess Diana's chart that the Moon at 25° Aquarius is Void in Course as the Moon does not make another aspect until reaching the next sign Pisces. The Moon then joins Mars who opposes from the 10th House. One sees here a difficulty between living privately and being a public person. (One could even say the public role, represented by Mars, "afflicted" Diana's private life.)

In a natal chart the Moon can bring the preceding and next planets together even if they do not aspect one another directly. If the Moon in Libra separates from a planet in Cancer and joins by sextile to a planet in Sagittarius, the Moon brings those two planets together. The Moon "translates" or "transfers" the light (or "virtue" or "nature") from the Cancer planet to the Sagittarius planet.

There is another species of application called "collection of light." Two planets do not even aspect each other but both join a planet slower than the other two and thus the two planets connect. The third heavier planet "collects the light" of the other two and thereby brings the two planets together. If, using the example in the previous paragraph, not the Moon but a ponderous planet is in Libra, the planets in Cancer and Sagittarius could both apply to that planet and be brought together in this way.

Because all classical planets can join another planet (even Saturn can join a stationary Mercury!), we must be careful in determining who is joining whom, what aspects become "perfect." Because the starry planets have variable rates of speed and all planets move easily from one sign to another, you need an ephemeris to be sure about many joining aspects in your chart. Horary astrologers know wonderful complexities that prevent aspects from perfecting.

A slower planet may go into the next sign before a faster planet perfects its aspect, and in the next sign another planet joins the slower planet or the slower planet joins a planet that's even slower. This is a "frustration," and some of us once experienced this in singles bars. A planet can "refrain" from perfecting an aspect to another: the faster planet applies to the slower planet but then goes retrograde and backs off. Here's another possibility: one planet (A) is about to join a slower one (B) but that slower planet (B) first joins a third planet (C) even slower than the second one (B). This is a "cutting off" or "abscission" of light. Astrologers can relate these planetary vicissitudes to specific situations in life and to general conditions of the native.

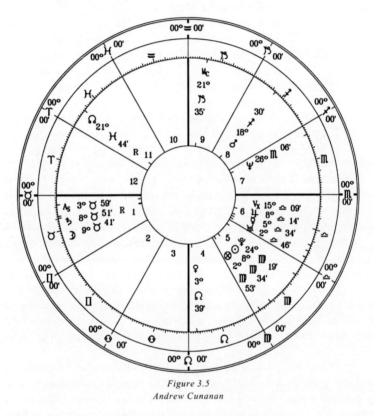

Figure 3.5
Andrew Cunanan

Let's look at another natal chart to illustrate another prevention of perfection that's called "prohibition," Andrew Cunanan (Aug. 31, 1969, 9:41 PM PDT, National City California 32N41, 117W05)[23] became notorious for an interstate spree in which he murdered former lovers from whom he may have contracted AIDS. His does not look like a problematic chart, especially considering that Moon was separating from Saturn when he was born. The Moon's next aspect is 15° away but it's a trine to Pluto.

Venus, the planet of sexual relationships, separates by sextile from Uranus. Venus is 03° Leo, Mercury is 05° Libra and Jupiter is 08° Libra. Before Venus can join Mercury, Mercury joins Jupiter and we might think that Venus will join Jupiter in this chart. This would be very good for Venus for Jupiter is the great benefic and a sextile is a harmonious aspect. Sadly, by the time Mercury joins Jupiter both planets have moved to 09° Libra so that Venus first joins Saturn at 08° by square! Saturn "prohibits" a sextile of the benefics to perfect itself. Sketching a story from the interplay of these planets, we see a pattern in relationships of great promise negated by bitter consequence.

Reception: Combining Joining and Disposition

The Medieval doctrine on reception is more complex than our modern version and is more dynamic. You can find the following doctrines in Guido Bonatti and Johannes Schoener.[24]

I think of reception, as articulated by the Medieval tradition, similar to feudalism or a protection racket. A planet applies to a planet in the dignities of the applying planet such as the Moon applies to a planet in Cancer or Taurus. The Moon thus "receives" the slower planet. The Moon "commits disposition, nature, and virtue" to the "received" planet, and the receiving planet can gain much. The faster planet needs help from the slower planet and commits its loyalty and resources (if it has any) to the slower planet who is in a position to increase its power and wealth. Receiving is only effective if the reception occurs by domicile or exaltation, as the Moon receiving a planet in Cancer or Taurus, or if the reception is by *two* of the minor dignities of triplicity, term, and face.

Reception between strong planets improves the aspect between the planets and may greatly improve what seems like a difficult square. In electional astrology you select a time for applying for a job when your significator receives the planet representing the party to whom you are applying. In horary astrology a reception between significators who join by favorable aspect signifies that the matter will have an easy and happy outcome. On the other hand, if the significators join by square with reception or sextile without reception, one predicts a favorable outcome but only after a struggle.[25]

In Princess Diana's natal chart Mercury in Cancer retrograde joins Mars in Virgo, and Mercury "receives" Mars as Mars is in Mercury's domicile. There's an interesting twist to this reception: not only is Mars in Mercury's dignities but Mercury is in the dignities of Mars! Look at the Table of Essential Dignities (page 10) and you will find that 03° Cancer, Diana's Mercury, is both the triplicity and term (or bound) of Mars. This is a kind of "mutual" reception that any Medieval astrologer would have noted.

Cunanan's chart gives us another example. Venus applies to Saturn in Taurus and Taurus is Venus's domicile. Does this make the square a bit easier? Note that Saturn is retrograde and is not happily placed in Taurus so the reception helps Saturn a little but does nothing for Venus.

A planet in debility cannot effectively receive another planet. If the Moon applies to a planet in Cancer or Taurus but she herself has poor disposition, is ill-natured and has no virtue, she may give her problems to the receiver. You won't find effective receptions between planets in signs that oppose one another for at least one of them will be in detriment and fall. If the Sun is in Aquarius and Saturn in Leo, or if Jupiter is in Capricorn and Mars in Cancer, do they improve each other by being in "mutual reception?" No! These planets in signs of their debility are too weak to help each other out.

Look for any receptions in your own natal chart where one planet joins another planet in the applying planet's dignities, and for receptions in which both planets receive each other. Do two planets have greater strength if together they aspect within moiety of their orbs and are in each others' major dignities? What if they receive each other but do not aspect at all? This final consideration is close to the Modern doctrine of mutual reception.

Modern astrology has departed from tradition in fundamental ways. We've added a myriad of new aspects based upon smaller and smaller proportions of the zodiac and upon non-zodiacal measurement. Viewing the zodiacal circle not as divided into discrete essential parts but as a continuum, any distance between two planets can now be some kind of relationship. Using midpoint configurations and planetary pictures, modern astrology explores a whole range of symmetries that, like aspects, describe connections between planetary energies. In all of these features the modern mind is at work developing its astrological understanding in modern ways.

The traditional doctrines on aspects are nonetheless part of today's astrology. Our field of study needs to understand traditional doctrines better and apply them consistently. Eventually we will assess older doctrines and modern developments and perhaps find ways to bring them together. Through examining issues such as aspects we understand astrology's needs for innovation and for continuity.

References and Notes

1. Ptolemy, *Tetrabiblos,* J.M. Ashmand, trans., (North Hollywood, CA.: Symbols and Signs, 1976), 121.

2. See Firmicus Maternus, *Book Four.* After previously delineating many aspects between planets in *Book Three,* he discusses the Moon only in terms of her applications and separations. Maternus, *Ancient Astrology: Theory and Practice* J. R. Bram, trans., available through Ballantrae Reprints, 1975.

3. I am using the Sagittarius rising chart for Princess Diana. In my opinion, this chart appears far more accurate than the other candidate.

4. The subdivisions of the circle were considered to be "ideal" forms that existed above and beyond the physical universe and which in turn generated the physical universe. The physical universe in its turn was believed to exhibit the influences of these forms in an approximate or even "corrupt" manner. But the signs and other recognized zodiacal subdivisions were part of the ideal more than the physical. This is a viewpoint that comes from Platonism, Pythagoreanism, and Hermeticism.

5. Dorotheus, Orpheus, et. al., *Teachings on Transits,* R. Schmidt, trans., (Berkeley Springs WV: Golden Hind Press, 1995).

6. This brings us to a problem which could have been a good reason for the Hellenistic tradition not to emphasize transits. Does an ingress *count* if the transiting planet goes back into the previous sign by retrogradation? This happens quite often, of course, and is one argument for considering an outer planet's heliocentric position.

7. Ptolemy, *Tetrabiblos, Book I,* R. Schmidt, trans., (Berkeley Springs, WV: Golden Hind Press, 1994), 29-30. In the Ashmand translation of Ptolemy, this is Ch 16.

8. Ibn Ezra, *The Book of Reasons,* Meira Epstein, trans., (Berkeley Springs WV: Golden Hind Press, 1994).

9. There is no other way of dividing the diameter of a circle into an even number of parts such that the lines drawn perpendicular to the diameter at these points also create a whole number division of the circumference of the circle. [Ed.]

10. Ptolemy, *Tetrabiblos, Book I,* R. Schmidt, trans., Berkeley Springs WV: Golden Hind Press, 1994), Ch 18. In the Ashmand translation, this is Ch 20. Bonatti also writes about this in the 13th Century in *Liber Astronomiae, Part II,* R. Zoller, trans., (Berkeley Springs WV: Golden Hind Press, 1994).

11. Maternus, *Ancient Astrology: Theory and Practice* J. R. Bram, trans., available through Ballentrae Reprints, 1975.

12. See Lehman, *Classical Astrology for Modern Living,* (Atgen, PA.: Whitford Press, 1996). In Chapter 9, Lehman uses these criteria to distinguish between "beholding" and "non-beholding" semi-sextiles and quincunxes. Her approach, which merits further investigation and testing, uses aspects within modern orbs. This is different from the ancient approach which would consider planets within these signs having aspect, regardless of the degrees within respective signs.

13. David Stricker (personal communication, 10/97) is investigating aspect words about seeing and perceiving and those such as "testifying" and "giving witness." that are about speaking. In Stricker's opinion these words relate to when a planet is above the horizon, or at least appearing on the oriental horizon, and when a planet is invisible below the horizon. It seems that the distinction had become lost by the time of the extant writings of the tradition.

14. R. Schmidt, personal communication, Oct. 1996.

15. Vettius Valens, *The Anthology, Book II, Part I,* R. Schmidt, trans.,Berkeley Springs WV: Golden Hind Press, 1994).

16. In *Liber Astronomiae Vol. III,* Bonatti raises the issue of conjunction by latitude and then dismisses it. This appears at the time to be upon the fringe of astrological speculation.

17. Lilly, *Christian Astrology,* Regulus Reprints, 1985, 157, 220. The horary example was on purchasing the house from "Master B".

18. See Guido Bonatti's "146 Considerations," rendered into English as *The Astrologer's Guide (Anima Astrologiae),* William Lilly and Henry Coley, eds. This work is now available from Ballentrae Press and JustUs Assoc.

19. Al-Biruni, *Book of Instruction in the Elements of the Art of Astrology.* R. W. Wright, trans., (1934) 255. Two different lists of planetary orbs are found in Lilly, *Christian Astrology,* 107, taken from his experience and from other astrologers. For a discussion of planetary orbs of light, see Ibn Ezra, *The Book of Reasons,* M. Epstein, trans., (Berkeley Springs WV: Golden Hind Press, 1994).

20. See Hand, introduction to Guido Bonatti, *Liber Astronomiae, Book III,* (Berkeley Springs WV: Golden Hind Press 1995).

21. When does a planet separate from another after perfection? The clearest statement I've seen is from Lilly, *Christian Astrology,* 110. He states that when the faster planet is six minutes of longitude away (bodily or by ray) from the slower planet, that faster planet is separating.

22. Lilly, *Christian Astrology,* 536

23. R. Hand on Cunanan's natal chart. Personal communication, Aug. 1997. Chart information courtesy of T. Lamb.

24. Guido Bonatti, *Liber Astronomiae, Tractatus III, Part II, Ch 13,* R. Hand, trans., and Johannes Schoener, *Opusculum Astrologicum, Canon 46,* R. Hand, trans., (Berkeley Springs WV: Golden Hind Press, 1994).

25. Guido Bonatti, *Liber Astronomiae, Part IV,* R. Hand, trans., (Berkeley Springs WV: Golden Hind Press, 1996) Ch 2.

Chapter 4: Planets as Significators in Ancient Astrology

Planets are the building blocks for all astrological work. In this chapter we will see how ancient astrologers worked with the seven classical planets, Sun through Saturn. Did the ancients describe planets in the same way as we do? There are some interesting variations.

Traditional natal astrology used planets to give pictures of specific areas of life. Sometimes the planets themselves refer to an area of life, *e.g.,* the Sun refers to one's father and the Moon to one's mother. For other issues, such as one's character or vocation, one finds a planet (and often a supporting planet) among several candidates within the chart. In modern astrology when we seek the ruler of a house for indications about an area of life signified by that house, we are finding a significant planet from within a chart. Every planet does not weigh in on every issue in a chart; one must seek the appropriate planets for the appropriate issues.

Warning — this chapter contains graphic descriptions of astrological outcomes! You may find some of these rather weird. Working with ancient astrology is much like learning about modern art and musical composition: upon working through some initial discomfort great riches remain.

Planets: Meaning and Use

When attending astrology conferences your name tag sometimes asks you to fill in the zodiacal signs of your Sun, Moon, and Ascendant. As a way to describe an individual this would never occur to an ancient astrologer! Instead, one might ask, "Are you Saturnine, Jovial, Mercurial?" (I guess we can no longer call a person "Venereal" or "Martian" without causing upset.) Before Myers-Briggs and before the Enneagram were the planets and our astrology. Much modern astrology depends on the personalities of the zodiacal signs. Ancient astrology, much like Uranian astrology and Cosmobiology, is strongly focused on the planets.

Although the basic definitions are similar, ancient astrologers didn't describe planets as we do, for example, that Mercury is thinking, Saturn is limitation, Uranus is the desire for freedom, etc. The Greeks used words from the root "sema" (σημα), a sign, mark, or token. A planet doesn't "mean" anything but "gives signs for," "signals," or "announces." (The Greeks also describe a planet "causing" or "producing" certain effects although it is not yet clear how they meant this.) A planet's use is not limited to one sphere of inquiry but encompasses many, and any single definition or defined area would limit that planet's functioning.

As you will see, each planet does have a character that you, the modern astrological reader, will recognize, yet that character is not one idea but many ideas which cannot be easily reduced to one another.[1]

As modern astrology students and teachers we sometimes over-identify a planet with one function it carries, usually a psychological one, and use this function as the planet's fundamental meaning. When interpreted poorly, planets are no longer symbols but simply placeholders for our own concepts.

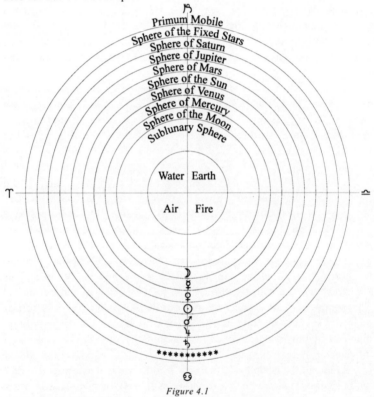

Figure 4.1

This is a representation of the cosmos based upon the observation and thinking of the ancients. The Earth is a fixed center around which the Moon, the planets, and the zodiac are arranged as spheres. The planets arranged from the outermost (Saturn) to closest (Moon) are in the "Chaldean Order," the traditional sequence of the planets.

Because planets have their intrinsic domains of use, because they are connected with zodiacal signs (through rulership and dignity), and because they modify other planets through being in aspect, we see that planets have their own patterns of activity. What are these patterns to the ancient astrologer?

Planets, Intrinsically

For natal astrology I rely on Ptolemy's *Tetrabiblos* (Ashmand translation)[2] and Vettius Valens (*Book I* of *The Anthology*).[3] I am particularly interested in matters of character and of employment. Both Vettius Valens and Ptolemy lived in the 2nd Century C.E.

Valens' extant work, *The Anthology*, provides us with a staggering amount of detail and application from the astrology of the Greco-Roman world. Ptolemy's *Tetrabiblos,* although more theoretical, is the most influential single work in astrology's history.

Sources I used for ancient horary and electional astrology are a book of excerpts entitled *Astrological Record of the Early Sages in Greek,*[4] and a few pages from Antiochus of Athens.[5]

We will look at the planets in the traditional "Chaldean Order," from the slowest-moving planet farthest away from earth (Saturn) to the fastest-moving planet and the one nearby (Moon). (See Figure 4.1)

Saturn, when positioned well in a natal chart and when he is the planet that describes a person's character, brings about what we would consider a "Capricorn type" — austere, serious and deep in thought, hard working and righteous, taciturn and solitary. For employment Saturn not only indicates laborers and farmers (Saturn also has authority over the earth), but also tax and custom collectors (Saturn bearing bad news?). Saturn also stands for people whose work is different from their interest or inclination.

Centuries before the movie *On the Waterfront* Saturn was associated with work around docks and harbors. At this time nobody understands this: do you have any ideas?

Saturn has to do with aspects of life that are disappointing or degraded in some matter. This feature of Saturn comes out when applied to horary questions in which you ask a question and the heavens answer back. In a question about a lost item Saturn indicates the item will be old, unfinished, or dirty. In a question about a thief if Saturn is in the 10th or 4th Sign from the Ascendant, the thief will betray himself. This quality of Saturn has not survived into modern astrology.

Generally speaking, a prominent Saturn in an event chart is very bad news. Upon the receipt of a letter, if Saturn is rising or culminating, the letter contains some terrible news, and if Saturn is also stationary, the letter may contain news about some constraints.

In an election chart the Moon in favorable aspect to Saturn is good for building and planting; in other aspects it signifies obstacles, oppositions, futility.

Valens sets down Saturn as ruler of ignorance and necessity; ignorance in the sense of stepping down from reason and becoming clouded, and necessity because Saturn constrains. The sphere of Saturn is also the farthest from the luminaries, and the domicile signs of Saturn (Capricorn, Aquarius) oppose those of the luminaries (Cancer, Leo). Hence the darkness we associate with Saturn.

Is Saturn so bad? Not in a natal chart if Saturn is an important significator. Here you may see qualities that assume a difficult world: gravity, frugality, and reserve. These virtues allow one to overcome all kinds of adversity.

Jupiter, unlike our modern treatment, is not the intellectual or the philosopher — this distinction belongs more to Mercury. Jupiter is more of an attitude or a presence, similar to Jupiter's long, slow, and luminous march across the heavens. When Jupiter is dignified, this soul is generous, gracious, lofty, and pious; when Jupiter is not well-dignified, he shines with a dimmer light. Jupiter is never difficult on his own. Valens stresses Jupiter's sociability, and a "jovial" character has friends and community.

There is little evidence that the ancients correlated Jupiter with arrogance, megalomania, or unrealistic expectations; this addition appears to have come later.

Jupiter gives few career indications. When configured with other planets, however, Jupiter tends one toward administration and business, or being priests and religious authorities. Jupiter makes larger and more magnificent what he contacts. Saturn, on the other hand, diminishes or spoils.

In an election Jupiter is "good for everything," especially alliances, approaching judges, and conducting business.[6] The Moon applying to a square or opposition to Jupiter does not alter the beneficence of that planet. If you get a letter and Jupiter is prominent, the letter contains great news.

Valens calls Jupiter the ruler of "opinion and crowns of office and will." Here we recognize Jupiter's characteristic faith and sense of enterprise.

With **Mars** life gets more energetic and far more problematic. Valens calls Mars the planet of action and troubles. When Mars operates well in a chart, he signifies a noble but irascible and daring character, the good guy in a modern action movie. When poorly-placed, Mars signifies the bad guy in a modern action movie: "He makes men cruel, mischievous, sanguinary, tumultuous, extravagant in expense, boisterous, ruffian-like, precipitate, drunken, rapacious, [etc.]" A poorly-placed Mars allied with Venus points to sexual license; allied with Mercury, Mars points to liars and thieves.

What are some occupational meanings of Mars? Mars brings us the military class and fighters, but also occupations which work with fire (in the kitchen as well as the smith or the factory). Accompanying Saturn, Mars will work underground in mines or keep animals or be a butcher.

If you get a letter with Mars in the 1st or 10th Signs from the Ascendant, this letter contains a great plot against you; if Mars is at station, the letter depicts a great struggle and the destruction of your superiors. If there is a stolen item and Mars is prominent, the theft occurred through violence and a break-in that destroyed property.

In an election the Moon applying to Mars by sextile or trine is good for activities of war, contest, home renovation, hunting, and being away from home (to defend oneself?). Other applying aspects of the Moon to Mars including the conjunction bring on opposition, violence, and futility.

The **Sun** is the central planet in the seven planetary spheres and is the luminary of the daytime. Valens gives this planet esoteric significations, calling the Sun the planet of light (in contrast to Saturn being ignorance and necessity), and the "light of the mind, the organ of perception of the soul." The Sun is the indication of our intelligent consciousness (Greek *nous*) within the planetary domain.

The specific character of the Sun is more difficult to come by. Ptolemy states that the Sun and Moon only contribute to a person's character when they are with other planets. If the Sun is well-placed in a chart, he contributes honor and glory, if poorly-placed, the opposite. There is no "solar" temperament as such. Ptolemy does not mention the Sun as a factor in one's work; Valens gives the Sun some qualities we associate with Jupiter: leadership, friendship, public authority.

In seeking a lost item Erasistratos mentions that when the luminaries are involved in the horary chart, the item is in front of one's eyes or in a bright place. This would not be true if the Sun and Moon are together in the 4th House: in that case a stolen item would be well-concealed.

In an election the Moon applying to the Sun by sextile and trine is good for consorting with the great (your next job interview?) and making contracts. Other applying aspects of Moon to Sun indicate opposition and contentiousness.

Venus, a brilliant and beautiful star when visible above the horizon, shows lovers of the arts, people who enjoy life and good things, who are agreeable in behavior and in speech. When poorly placed, Venus gives testimony for dullness, voluptuousness, sordidness, and quaking shyness. As the indicator of career or action Venus signifies people who work with gold, ornaments, and other beautiful things, or who are musicians and artists.

When configured with other planets, Venus also signifies the involvement or the favor of women, or a sexual dimension to an issue. If you get a letter with Venus prominent in the heavens, it was probably written by a woman and is probably favorable. In a lost item chart Venus and the Moon mean a woman owns the items. In an electional chart the Moon's application to Venus is great for marriage and love-affairs of all kinds. It's also good for social occasions, beautifying and redecorating, and showing kindness.

Mercury gives us some surprises. Mercury is more the intellectual planet than we moderns think; he is the planet that rules astrologers and diviners of all kinds. Valens brings Mercury into line with "law, custom, and fidelity."

A mercurial personality can be inventive, prudent, thoughtful, and skillful in argument. Mercury's quickness can also be a disadvantage: "He makes men busy in all things, precipitate, forgetful, variable, regretful, foolish, inconsiderate, void of truth, careless, inconstant. . ."

Mercury, the elusive quick planet in the skies, had some significations that we now give to Uranus.

Mercury's vocational choices are among writers, businessmen, astrologers, merchants and bankers. Valens adds mimes, orators, architects, and those who interpret dreams, literature or teachings.

Mercury has another quality that is important, his ability to blend in anywhere. Mercury makes favorable configurations better and unfavorable ones worse. When Mercury is problematic, he produces baseness, vulgarity.[7] The Moon applying to Mercury is good for scientific work, transcribing and translating, and sending things to another place.

The **Moon** is a more neutral planet than in modern astrology. In natal astrology the Moon adds testimonies of mother or women when that is relevant to an issue. In ancient electional and horary astrology the condition of the Moon is crucial. Whereas the Sun is in many ways an administrator of a chart, the Moon indicates the flow of time. The situation of the Moon indicates the nature of the present moment and its movement into the conditions of the future.

Does the Moon have intrinsic qualities? It appears that the ancients used the Lot of Fortune for many of the qualities we might associate with the Moon. Ptolemy hints at other possibilities that are closer to the modern astrological temperament. The Moon, according to Ptolemy, has to do with the sensitive and irrational mind, Mercury with the intellectual mind. In *Book IV* of *The Tetrabiblos* Ptolemy tells us that the Moon, in the "place of action," "produces soothsayers, diviners, interpreters of dreams, and magicians."[8]

Now we begin to apply the planets systematically. Ancient astrological writers routinely gave general principles for assessing a planet's condition and then gave many examples of its use. Ancient astrological teachings force the student (and modern reader) to grapple with and contemplate a wide range of applications and possibilities, not as a set of concepts, but as images or pictures. A different kind of astrological insight, perhaps a more creative one, unfolds over time.

A Sample Astrology Lesson

In *Book II* of *The Anthology*, Chapter 17, Valens describes Mercury trine Mars or sextile Mars.[9] Valens specifies not inner states of mind but outer manifested experience.

> [It] is indicative of diverse kinds of work: sometimes scribes, other times merchants, interpreters, geometers, lawyers, philosophers, but all are malignant, cunning, clever, false. And it also makes arms instructors or those who juggle with weapons.[10]

These people use a strong intellect for their work (Mercury) but in an aggressive or self-serving way (Mars). Valens gives us diversity and possibility; implicitly, we can now supply some of our own. One difference is clear: a modern astrologer may think Jupiter, not Mercury, is more the planet of lawyers and philosophers. Valens now discusses

Jupiter.

> And if the star of Zeus [Jupiter] should also be configured, especially in profitable *zoidia,* it makes those who are soldierly, and often augurers, sacrificers, those who foresee the future, those who perceive the odder things about men.[11]

How does a well-placed Jupiter influence Mercury and Mars? Jupiter gives these planets wider scope and a tendency to operate more beneficially. Now let's see how the square between Mars and Mercury (without the benefic rays of Jupiter) can operate.

> And the square will make a greater diversity of the aforementioned: for, it makes wizards, impostors, sacrificers, astrologers, those who court the mob, money-changers, counterfeiters, those who conduct their business by villainy and attacks and cunning. And they also become thieves and perjurers and those who are impious and plotters of similar things. . .[12]

Valens never tells you what a square is but what it does. Note how morally neutral these delineations are. A square does not necessarily signal difficulty but that the planets will operate more powerfully, for good or ill. Now Valens gives us more possibilities based upon house placement for Mercury and Mars.

> And especially when they happen in the subterraneous *zoidion* [4th House] or Descendant or if the one should be setting while the other subterraneous, they will bring about murders or they will be accomplices and make their living by robbery. And some will be fratricides, and their final end will be violent, especially if they also help the Moon. For they become those who die violent deaths and are unburied.[13]

Why are these delineations now so negative? The 4th and 7th Houses are angular and are still powerful, yet not as positive as the other angular houses, the 1st and 10th. Why fratricides? Mercury has to do with young people, especially brothers, and Mars, of course, can be a violent planet. By "going negative" Valens illustrates a certain range of possibilities.

Ancient astrologers, more than modern astrologers, describe extreme outcomes for birthchart factors. One aspect alone does not make a fraud or augurer or fratricide! Many other chart factors must agree. We modern astrologers tend to make our descriptions more neutral and then consider the evolution of the individual. Ancient astrologers are not a gruesome lot, yet they are more direct about how difficult some chart factors are, and how difficult personal evolution is.[14] Also, life was generally more difficult and survival more an issue.

Valens' delineation leaves out an important question: how do you apply a chart factor, like a Mercury-Mars contact, to a natal chart? Indeed, what he has given us is an abstract exercise. I will try to answer that question below.

Significators in a Natal Chart

A basic principle of traditional natal astrology, understood by modern horary and electional astrologers, is that a chart is unintelligible unless you ask it a question. The act of asking a question gives form and meaning to an astrological configuration. For the above Mercury-Mars contact to signify something, we need to know the matter of concern.

After formulating a question or concern, the astrologer frequently works the chart to find a *significator* for a specific issue. Instead of whirling around charts of serial killers (another negative example of Mercury-Mars?), one first sets up astrological criteria to assess serial killing, and judges relevant charts accordingly.[15] This way we can see the range of astrological outcomes.

Planets as Natural Significators: Love and Marriage

Certain planets naturally speak to specific issues of life: the Sun for issues of father or for authority and rank, the Moon for mother, Venus for relationships and sexuality, and Jupiter for wealth.

Again, let's turn to Vettius Valens, who at the end of *Book II* of *The Anthology* discusses conjugal bliss or its lack.[16] We see how the various planets when configured with the natural significator Venus tell us about matters of marriage. Again, instead of tendencies or states of mind, Valens gives us images and stories.

If Venus is in or has dealings with "bicorporeal" or what we call "mutable" zodiacal signs, and if Mercury is also involved with Venus, especially at night (Sun below the horizon, so that Venus is in sect and stronger[17]), the outcome is polygamy and license. Mercury is about variety and multiplicity as are "bicorporeal" or mutable signs, and we get a love-life that is multiple. And if Mars is also involved? "Intercourse with many male children!" Why male children? Mercury "gives signs for young people," Mars for men, Venus for sexuality.

How does a powerful Saturn influence Venus in matters of marriage? This is a personal concern to me! Valens gives two scenarios.

If Saturn is a strong dispositor of Venus or in opposition by ascensional times[18] and no other planets are weighing in, then Venus is wholly influenced by Saturn. The result? "They will be widows and virgins."[19] Saturn cuts off from sexuality, gives sterility. If Mars were also there, this configuration could signify intercourse with men, or Jupiter could add fertility, or Mercury would add opportunity or, at the least, make one excited by young people.

Here is Valens' other scenario. If Saturn is in the 10th Sign from Venus (considered a predomination), or if Saturn opposes Venus zodiacally, and especially if Mercury is aspecting, Saturn will "cool and defile the marriage." Mercury, it seems, would also help cool or defile a marriage due to somebody's wandering eye or desire to have many young lovers.

We modern astrologers, bred in a Freudian age, are more accustomed to seeing Saturn as inhibition, neurotic restraint, and a drying out of emotion or liveliness. Ancient writings reflect this, yet there is another outcome of Saturn — corruption or defilement. I think of this in light of ancient astro-theology: the outermost visible sphere of the fixed stars is stable and unchanging; yet upon Saturn, that cold dim planet, we are into the realm of change and corruption. This may remind the modern reader of Pluto.

(If you have a Saturn-Venus contact in your chart, or are in love with someone who does, do not lose all hope! Remember that Saturn assumes a difficult world, and, acting accordingly, can have positive manifestations: a sense of seriousness and responsibility.)

Valens gives us another kind of scenario for Venus based upon a planet "setting under the beams." When a planet moves close to the Sun in its zodiacal path, that planet will disappear into the light of the Sun. "If [Mars] and [Venus] should have set under the beams, the natives will engage in clandestine adulteries and secret sins. And if they should also happen to be oriental [rising before the Sun] or upon pivot points [angular houses], it will be more apparent." Hopefully, Jupiter can save the day by aspecting Venus and Mars! Saturn would certainly ruin it.

In electional astrology, modern and ancient, it is good to begin something clandestine when the Moon is hidden by the beams of the Sun. Angularity, however, implies that something will manifest in a stronger or more obvious way.

64

Valens then tells us the many ways in which Venus and Mars, signaling clandestine adulteries and secret sins, lead to disaster. I will spare the reader these grim details.

There is, fortunately, some happiness to be found in married life. If you have Venus strongly placed and in good aspect from Jupiter, that augurs not only personal happiness but material benefit. (If, however, Mercury comes on the scene, watch out for promiscuity and inconstancy!)

Derived Significators

No specific planet has natural dominion over character and work, or personality and career. That planet must be found from within each chart. One frequently finds the strongest planet in a position sensitive to an area of life, and then uses that planet to describe the area of life. The condition of that significant planet will give indications of success or failure in that area. By the time of the Renaissance finding different "Almutens" — or planetary lords — for different areas of life became enormously complicated.[20]

Today we typically use a simpler system, casting a ruler of a specific house as significator for an issue. For example, if Scorpio is on my 2nd House cusp, then Mars is a significator for money and finances (Jupiter will have some natural dominion as well). You will see how sophisticated ancient astrology is in these matters.

Planetary Lord of "Soul" — Character or Personality Style

Occasionally I ask students, "If you were a planet, which planet would you be? Who would be in second place?" The responses are always lively and interesting. Planets, interpreted according to astrology, are not concepts but personalities that we can experience directly. Here I leave aside the question of an overall planetary "ruler of a chart," but instead find the planet that resonates with us psychologically.

Ptolemy in *Tetrabiblos III,* Chapter 18, gives us a deceptively simple technique to find the "lord of the soul" — the dispositor (that planet with the most essential dignities) over the places of the Moon and Mercury in the birthchart. These are the dignities of domicile, exaltation, triplicity, and term or bound, and another he calls phase. In addition to looking for the dispositors of the Moon and Mercury, one looks to these planets themselves — their zodiacal signs, aspects from the Sun, and whether they are at angles.

65

Why the Moon and Mercury? Mercury is the reasoning mind, and the Moon the more sensitive and irrational qualities. Together they give you a planet or planets which give signs for one's basic character.

Ptolemy's is a straightforward technique, yet applying it requires imagination and analysis. A computer program cannot do this for you!

Here is a sample delineation of planetary character using the nativity of someone well-known in this writer's professional and personal life, his wife. (See Figure 4.2)

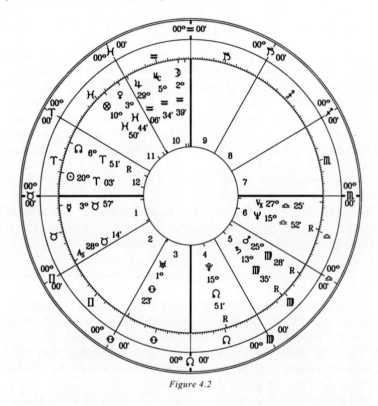

Figure 4.2

Looking for the "Lord of the Soul" in this chart. (Answer: Venus, and also Saturn)

The intellectual soul is represented by Mercury which is in Jill-laurie's 1st House using a whole-sign chart. At the 4th degree of Taurus Mercury is in the domicile, triplicity, and bounds of Venus. Venus is herself strongly dignified (in exaltation sign) in the 11th House of the

Good Spirit, and oriental to the Sun. Importantly, Mercury is in exact sextile to his dispositor, Venus. (This is a "reception," as discussed previously in Chapter 3, page 51, and medieval astrologers make much of it.) According to Ptolemy,

> When Venus rules alone in a position of glory, she renders the mind benignant, good, voluptuous, copious in wit, pure, gay, fond of dancing, jealous, abhorring wickedness, delighting in the arts, pious, modest, well-disposed. . .[21]

One cannot ignore the Moon, especially since the Moon squares Mercury in this chart. The Moon is also in an angular house, and is close to the Midheaven degree. The lord of the Moon is (using the traditional ruler for Aquarius) Saturn, which is retrograde and strongly configured: Saturn opposes the Lot of Fortune and also Venus, the dispositor of Mercury. Mars, known as a malefic, is also in Virgo.

Our rosy forecast based on the strong Venus is clouded by this more difficult Saturn. If Saturn is a significator and is not in glory, there are untoward consequences. "He will debase the mind, making it penurious, pusillanimous, ill-disposed, indiscriminating, malignant, timorous, slanderous, fond of solitude. . ."[22]

Putting these factors together, the nativity describes a kind, friendly, and joyful person who has also had to work through anxiety and depression. As the Moon has more to do with the nonrational mind, Jill-laurie is likely to have a Venus-like outer character with a Saturn undertow. Saturn, then as now, knows how to ruin a good time! The strength of Mercury and Venus, however, indicates a positive outcome, and indeed this has been the case over time.

Finding the planet or planets of soul, personality, or character has been important to astrology for centuries. Around 900 C.E., Masha'allah was a Jewish astrologer in the Arab world who used a strongly Hellenistic approach to his art. In his *Book of Nativities*[23] Masha'allah looks for the signs of the Ascendant and Mercury, the lords of those positions, and their respective placement in a birthchart.

In a more sophisticated exposition from the 14th Century, Antonio de Montulmo[24] examines the lords (Almutens) of the Ascendant, Moon, and Mercury one at a time and with other factors to ascertain three qualities of soul: vegetative, sensitive, and intellectual. The chart above may be more completely examined using Montulmo's methods.

Renaissance authorities used the Almuten of Mercury, Moon, and Ascendant, the Almuten being the planet that scores the most points in a position or many positions, according to the five categories of dignity.

The Planetary Lord of Action or Career

How does one find the planet or planets important to career? Here we are not looking at one's job, but literally the "quality of action." (The Greek word is *praxis*, actually close to the Sanskrit *karma*.) We might now call it one's life-work or activity of life; yet we see that these planets pertain to employment.

Both Paulus Alexandrinus (4th Century C.E.) and Ptolemy give criteria for finding a planet, or a proper mixture of planets, most relevant to career issues. Both prefer Mercury, Venus, and Mars, as do most others.

Paulus Alexandrinus in Chapter 26 of *Introductory Matters* says that one first looks for a house proper to career issues, or at least one that helps a planet be effective in this function.

Do Mercury, Venus, or Mars fall in a house profitable for one's action? The 10th House (tenth zodiacal sign from the Ascendant) is the best of the angular houses; the 2nd House the best of the succedent houses; the 6th House the best of the cadent.

If the Sun or Moon applies to Mars, Jupiter, or Saturn as its next aspect, or if one appears in the morning before dawn, that planet may be the significator for "action." If either Mercury or Venus rise in the evening (but not within the Sun's beams), that planet would be the stronger significator.

Ideal would be a planet in a strong house (one directly relevant to one's career) which is also the next application of the Sun or Moon, and a morning riser (if Mars, Jupiter, or Saturn), or an evening riser (if Venus or Mercury). Again, we're more interested in Mercury, Venus, and Mars.

What criteria does Ptolemy use? In *Tetrabiblos IV,* Chapter 4, he discusses the lord (*kurios*) of action. Ptolemy uses the Sun and the 10th Sign from the Ascendant (our Midheaven) to determine the quality of one's action. We look first for the planet that is within the culminating sign, or visibly rises just before the Sun (it must be at least 12° away from the Sun), particularly when that planet is the Moon's next approaching aspect. Only if no planets meet these criteria do you use the ruler of the Midheaven sign, but that may imply difficulty in this area.

If there are two planets that meet the criteria, choose the one that is more dignified but use the other in a secondary way. If, for example, both Mercury and Mars are candidates, and Mars is angular or in Aries, Scorpio, or Capricorn, Mars would have primary responsibility with Mercury assisting. This person could be a fighter with words instead of a hard-working writer.

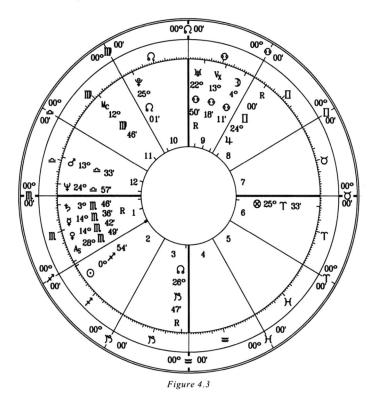

Figure 4.3

Look for the planet that tells about one's work. (Answer: Mercury)

Hephaistio of Thebes, from the 5th Century C.E., provides more detail that is consistent with Ptolemy.[25]

If Mercury, Venus and Mars do not appear in the 10th House, 4th House, 1st House, or the house of the Lot of Fortune, find the planet which is the Moon's next application.

If the Moon applies to none as her next aspect, use the planet nearest to the Sun, making a morning appearance (rising before the Sun).

Is Mercury, Venus, or Mars in the 6th House? Use that. As a last resort, use a planet in the 2nd House.

This examination will give you a planet that is the lord of one's Action. (See Figure 4.3 which is the birthchart of one of my recent clients.)

Using whole-sign houses, one notices both Venus and Mercury in the 1st House. These planets naturally and in the chart are clearly in the running as the lords of this person's action.

Neither Mercury nor Venus is the Moon's or Sun's next application; both the Sun and Moon apply to Mars! Yet Mars is in detriment in an unprofitable house, the 12th. Mars would stand poorly for the planet of one's action, but may be a secondary factor.

No classical planet is in the 10th Sign from the Ascendant sign. The ruler of the 10th Sign Leo is the Sun which is in the 2nd House, yet the Sun is not a planet we would want for this purpose. Mercury, however, is the ruler of the Midheaven degree, which is in Virgo. Mercury, along with Venus, is in close sextile to the Midheaven degree.

Which planet rises just before the Sun? Venus does, but is closely followed by Mercury in the same degree. One notices that Mercury is retrograde. It is also the case, however, that Mercury is emerging from the Sun's beams (it is stationary as the Sun moves away from it) and Venus is going into the Sun's beams (moving faster than the Sun, heading toward the Sun).

Because of Mercury's position in the 1st House, moving out of the Sun's beams, and as the sign ruler for the Midheaven degree, I am inclined to use Mercury as primary lord of my client's action.

My client has been an accountant and financial manager, a Mercury profession, for most of his working life. He received little formal training for this profession but has done well nonetheless. His original career choice was business administration (Mercury, again, with a touch of Jupiter), but his family situation prevented him from going to business school.

My client has been in the position of working the bottom line for companies that have not been profitable, and he has had to deliver the bad news to company owners. (Mars in the 12th House?) My client is completely unhappy about that part of his work.

Recently his company has encountered financial difficulties, entirely of its own creation, and my Mercurial client has had to witness this process and do his best under the difficult circumstances. Yet he is confident in his abilities. He feels that, if it is necessary, he can always start again elsewhere as an accountant and financial manager.

References and Notes

1. For an excellent contemporary discussion of the nature of planets and our astrological understanding, see the early chapters from Dennis Elwell's *Cosmic Loom,* (London: Unwin Hyman, 1987), Ch 2.

2. Ptolemy, *Tetrabiblos,* J. Ashmand, trans., (North Hollywood, CA: Symbols & Signs, 1976).

3. Vettius Valens, *The Anthology Book I,* R. Schmidt trans., (Berkeley Springs, WV: Golden Hind Press, 1994).

4. *Astrological Record of the Early Sages in Greek,* R. Schmidt trans., (Berkeley Springs, WV: Golden Hind Press, 1995).

5. Antiochus of Athens. *The Thesaurus,* R. Schmidt trans., (Berkeley Springs, WV: Golden Hind Press, 1993).

6. *Ibid,* 41.

7. Paulus Alexandrinus. *Introductory Matters,* R. Schmidt trans., (Berkeley Springs, WV: Golden Hind Press, 1995), 14.

8. Ptolemy, *Tetrabiblos,* Robbins, trans., (Cambridge: Loeb Classical Library, Harvard University Press, 1940), 391. This edition, although a weaker translation than Ashmand, supplies the Greek text. Robbins's phrase "place of action" is much closer to the text than Ashmand's "the place regulating the employment." Ashmand, 123.

9. Vettius Valens, *The Anthology Book II, Part I,* R. Schmidt trans., (Berkeley Springs, WV: Golden Hind Press, 1994) 24.

10. *Ibid.*

11. *Ibid.*

12. *Ibid.*

13. *Ibid.*

14. R. Hand, personal communication, 1995.

15. Pierce, D.K., "Reconciling Interpretative and Statistical Significance," *ISAR Journal, Vol.1,* 1995.

16. Vettius Valens. *The Anthology Book II (concl.)* & *Book III,* R. Schmidt, trans., (Berkeley Springs, WV: Golden Hind Press, 1994).

17. A planet of the nocturnal sect, Venus, Moon and Mars are considered more effective in a nighttime chart.

18. Ascensional aspects are not according to the fixed circle of the zodiac but the varying times a zodiacal sign rises for a latitude in question.

19. Vettius Valens. *The Anthology Book II (concl.)* & *Book III,* R. Schmidt, trans., (Berkeley Springs, WV: Golden Hind Press, 1994), 1.

20. Unpublished summary of Johannes Schoener. *Three Books on the Judgment of Nativities,* a planned future translation from ARHAT.

21. Ptolemy, *Tetrabiblos,* J. Ashmand, trans., (North Hollywood, CA: Symbols & Signs, 1976), 112.

22. *Ibid.,* 109.

23. Masha'allah. *The Book of Nativities,* R. Hand trans., (Berkeley Springs, WV: Golden Hind Press, 1994).
24. Antonio de Montulmo. *On the Judgment of Nativities, Part II,* R. Hand trans., (Berkeley Springs, WV: Golden Hind Press, 1995).
25. Unpublished translation by R. Schmidt.

Chapter 5: Planetary Sect

A Brief History of Sect

The Hellenistic tradition presents planetary sect as an important factor in assessing a planet in a birth chart. This doctrine consists of one criterion with additional factors. Ancient astrology values the Sun and diurnal planets in a daytime chart, the Moon and nocturnal planets in a nighttime chart: that's the one criterion. Authorities mention two other factors: placement with the Sun and diurnal and nocturnal planets being in masculine and feminine signs respectively. They did not, however, employ these other two factors consistently.

Medieval astrology puts all three together so that a planet that meets all three is, using the Arabic, in "Hayz" or "Aym" or in its own light. Medieval astrologers, however, used "Hayz" as one factor among many to assess a planet's condition in a birth chart, and not a very important one. Ancient astrologers valued planetary sect much more than their Medieval descendants.

The Medieval traditions also saw diurnal and nocturnal as masculine and feminine, confusing "sect" with "similitude." This brings problems when considering Mars: he is the ultimate masculine planet, but is given as a nocturnal planet.

Over time the role of planetary sect became very confused, and by the end of the Medieval tradition the practice of observing sect was dropped entirely. It has not been until recently, with the rediscovery of astrology's traditions, that astrologers have contemplated and begun testing this old doctrine. The doctrine of planetary sect in all its complexity has much to offer to modern astrological analysis, and I hope that you will try it out on your charts and those of others.

What is Planetary Sect?

The[1] Greek word *hairesis* means a "faction," as in a religious sect. (The word "heresy," once close in meaning to our word "sectarian," comes from *hairesis*.) The word "sect" comes from the Latin *seco* which means "to cut" or "divide." Therefore, sect is a division, and ancient astrology used two sects — diurnal and nocturnal, day and night. The Sun is the leader of the diurnal or daytime sect and the Moon is the leader of the nocturnal or nighttime sect. Day and night sect are similar to, but not identical to, masculine and feminine.

When a planet is in sect, the chart supports the expression of that planet; out of sect, a planet is out of step with its environment. The chart's "environment" is determined by 1) whether the chart is a day or night chart; 2) the position of a planet's placement in relationship to the Sun; and 3) the sign a planet inhabits.

To understand how a planet's sect is supported or not supported by the chart's environment imagine you are at a gathering of other astrologers — your fellow "sectarians." Here you can feel comfortable and express yourself spontaneously. If you were a planet, you would be "in sect." Next, imagine yourself in a gathering of self-appointed skeptics bemoaning the sorry state of human reason as shown by astrology's popularity. In such a gathering you would be less comfort-able, more defensive. You might be considered completely "outside of sect." However, if you were familiar with the Gauquelin studies or versed in philosophy or history of science, you'd find ways to make the evening interesting, or at least bearable. Here you would be like a planet only partially "outside of sect."

But why is planetary sect an important issue for modern astrolo-gers?

O   You will find that using these principles adds important information not otherwise found in modern birth chart delineation. In other words, this is a technique that works.

O   Sect provides another way to apply the feminine to a birth chart.

O   Planetary sect works closely with the essential dignities of planets, encouraging a new appreciation for the traditional system of dignities.

O   At the foundation of all astrology is the *appearance* of the moving sky, and planetary sect factors in the most obvious visual quality of the sky — whether it is daytime or nighttime.

O   Planetary sect helps us access the birth chart and its planets as a more immediate experience, where our insights are closer to sensation than to concept. By using planetary sect (along with the masculine and feminine, and the four qualities of hot, cold, wet, and dry), we get a special feel for a birth chart and its planets. The feel for the chart is as much bodily as it is mental, immediate and easy to communicate.

In terms of accessing the senses modern astrology comes close when using the four elements — fire, earth, air, water. Yet sect is where ancient astrology offers a more sophisticated and more powerful system. So now let's use the ordinary experience of day and night, the four qualities, and the masculine and feminine to better use our astrology.

Planets by Sect: Diurnal and Nocturnal

What happens during daytime? Until this century a person's activities changed radically with the sky's alternating brightness and darkness. During the day with the Sun above the horizon there is more activity and more work. One can see more clearly. In the daytime one can see the lines between objects better and can see colors more distinctly. The activities of the day are also more individual and more intentional. One's daytime social life is public, role-bound, and hierarchical.

During the night when the Sun is below the horizon, movements slow down and become quieter, more introspective, and more personal. When there is strong activity at night, the experience tends to be more communal, more imbued with feeling and sensation than intellect. (Notice, in our modern times, the tone of a modern city's "night life.")

Some planets flourish with the activities of daytime, others more in the nighttime. The Sun and Jupiter are clearly daytime planets and are enhanced in a diurnal environment. The Moon and Venus, closer to the activities of nighttime, are enhanced in a nocturnal chart. However, the malefic planets — Mars and Saturn — are in sect when conditions modify or balance their nature. Thus, the fiery nature of Mars is balanced by being nocturnal, while the coldness of Saturn is modified by being diurnal. Mercury, of course, is neutral.[2]

In descending order of diurnality, the diurnal planets are the Sun, Jupiter, and Saturn. The nocturnal planets are the Moon, Mars, and Venus. In a daytime chart the planets that are naturally in sect are the Sun, Jupiter, and Saturn. In a nighttime chart the Moon, Venus, and Mars are naturally in sect.

The sect of Mercury is determined by his position in relationship to the Sun. If Mercury rises before the Sun — comes earlier in the zodiac than the Sun — he is diurnal. If Mercury rises after the Sun — comes later in the zodiac than the Sun — he is nocturnal. Looking at the seven classical planets in the charts of Bill Clinton and Bob Dole, we see that both men have diurnal Mercuries.[3] (See Figures 5.1 and 5.2)

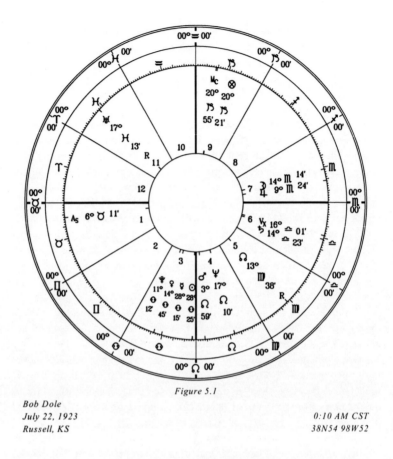

Figure 5.1

Bob Dole
July 22, 1923   0:10 AM CST
Russell, KS   38N54 98W52

Four Qualities — Dry, Hot, Wet, and Cold

In *Tetrabiblos I*, Chapter 11, Ptolemy (from the 2nd Century C.E.) relates the daily cycle to the qualities of dry, hot, wet, and cold, which come close to our experience of the different times of day.

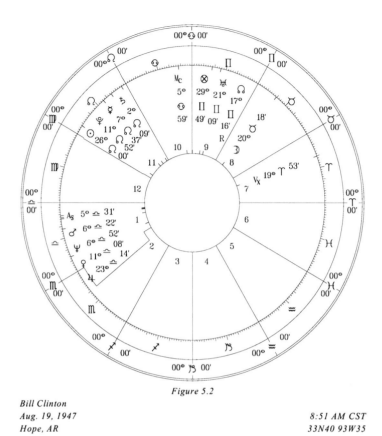

Figure 5.2

Bill Clinton
Aug. 19, 1947
Hope, AR

8:51 AM CST
33N40 93W35

At sunrise with the Sun at the Ascendant the quality *dry* predominates as the moisture that has accumulated at night dries off. Psychologically speaking dry is mentally alert. Dry is also analytical, detached, and discriminating. At midday with the Sun culminating *hot* predominates and our activity becomes energetic or frenzied. In a hot climate there is too much heat and people slow down to compensate.

Sunset features *wet* as dew begins to form. Wet allows separate things to come back together and relates to the flowing or floating experiences we have. We come home after a hard day at work and relax with our loved ones or we go out socially. Toward midnight, however, with the Sun anti-culminating the dominant quality is *cold*; cold reduces activity and allows things to come to rest.

The daytime then is dry and hot and the nighttime is wet and cold.

77

Daytime is separating and more energetic. Nighttime is more intuitive and more restful.

Masculine and Feminine

The four qualities along with daytime and nighttime are associated with the division of masculine and feminine. "The interval of the day happens to be more masculine because of the heat and vigor in it, but night is more feminine because of its moisture and gift of rest."[4] Zodiacal signs and planets have masculine or feminine qualities.

The masculine zodiacal signs are the fire triplicity, Aries, Leo, and Sagittarius, and the air triplicity, Gemini, Libra, and Aquarius. These signs all add a diurnal quality. The feminine signs are the earth triplicity, Taurus, Virgo, and Capricorn, and the water triplicity, Cancer, Scorpio, and Pisces. These signs add a nocturnal quality.[5]

The masculine planets are the Sun, Saturn, Jupiter, and Mars. The feminine planets are the Moon and Venus. Mercury, of course, is neutral. Notice, however, that Mars is a nocturnal planet by sect and a masculine planet by gender.

Determining Chart and Planetary Sect

In determining sect there are three criteria that the ancients followed, and these are easily defined. First and foremost, is the chart diurnal or nocturnal? Second, the planet's placement in relationship to the Sun affects its diurnality or nocturnality. And third, whether the planet is in a masculine or feminine sign also affects its diurnality or nocturnality. Following are explanations of these three criteria, as well as how sect enhances or strengthens a planet in one's chart.

Criterion #1: Are You a Day Person or a Night Person?
If the Sun is below the horizon, your chart is a nocturnal chart. If your Sun is above the horizon, your chart is diurnal. If you were born during the daytime, as was President Clinton, then the Sun, Jupiter, and Saturn, and maybe Mercury, are naturally in sect, and the other planets are out of sect. If you were born at night, like former Senator Dole, then the Moon, Venus, Mars, and maybe Mercury, are naturally in sect, while the others are out of sect. In Bill Clinton's chart the diurnal planets automatically become expressive. In Bob Dole's chart the nocturnal planets have support.

Criterion #2: Is the Planet with the Sun or Not with the Sun?

While the position of the Sun determines whether the chart is diurnal or nocturnal, a planet's placement relative to the Sun affects its diurnality or nocturnality. Vettius Valens from the 2nd Century C.E. described how a planet could be more strongly in sect. (We see an almost identical passage in Antiochus of Athens, a later author).[6]

It is also necessary to consider the sect of the stars, for the Sun, Zeus, and Kronos rejoice when they are above the earth during the day, below the earth at night. But the Moon, Ares, and Aphrodite rejoice when they are above the earth at night, and below the earth at day.[7]

In *Night and Day* Rob Hand calls this "sect by placement." The Sun prefers being above the horizon, for that is the criterion of daytime. As diurnal planets Jupiter, Saturn, and (diurnal) Mercury prefer being on *the same side* of the horizon with the Sun. Thus, diurnal placement for any planet, whether it be a diurnal or nocturnal planet, is either above the horizon with the Sun in a day chart or below the horizon with the Sun in a night chart. Conversely, the nocturnal Moon, Venus, Mars, and (nocturnal) Mercury prefer to be on the *other side* of the horizon from the Sun — below the horizon during the day, above the horizon at night. Thus, nocturnal placement for any of the planets is below the horizon during the day, and above the horizon at night.

This leads to an interesting conclusion, also mentioned by Valens. *Only planets above the horizon can be completely in sect naturally and by placement.* During the day when the Sun is above the horizon, the diurnal planets enjoy being on the same side as the Sun. Clinton's Sun, Mercury and Saturn are completely in sect — diurnal planets on the same side as the Sun (above the horizon). And because nocturnal planets enjoy being on the other side of the Sun, when the Sun is below the horizon (at night), nocturnal planets completely in sect must be above the horizon away from the Sun. In Dole's chart only the Moon is completely in sect — a nocturnal planet above the horizon, on the other side from the Sun.

However, when nocturnal planets are placed diurnally (same side as the Sun) or diurnal planets are placed nocturnally (below the horizon), the planets have mixed indicators of sect. For example, in Bob Dole's nighttime chart, Venus, Mars, and Saturn are diurnally placed, but Venus and Mars are nocturnal planets. Thus, Venus and Mars become less completely in sect, while Saturn becomes more in sect. Saturn, a diurnal planet, "rejoices," but not Venus and Mars for they are nocturnal by nature. When we think of Dole's public demeanor, we think more of Saturn than we do of Venus or Mars.

Conversely, in Bill Clinton's daytime chart Venus, Mars, and Jupiter are nocturnally placed, but Jupiter is a diurnal planet. Since Venus and Mars are nocturnally placed, they become more in sect while diurnal Jupiter which is nocturnally placed becomes less. Venus and Mars are enhanced. Jupiter is not.

Look at former Senator Dole's chart again. Note that the Moon and Jupiter are above the horizon in his 7th House. As mentioned before, the Moon is naturally in sect (a nocturnal planet in a nocturnal chart). Furthermore, since his Moon is on the other side of the horizon from the Sun (thus nocturnally placed), she becomes even more in sect. In this favorable situation his Moon has probably given him emotional strength to overcome adversity.

On the other hand, Dole's Jupiter, which is naturally diurnal, is nocturnally placed across the horizon from the Sun. Therefore, Jupiter does not "rejoice" as much. In Dole's chart we already get a feel for the Moon's emotional and subjective strength, and Jupiter's relative quiescence and modesty.

Dole's Moon in her fall in Scorpio does not lend itself to easy emotional self-expression, and could make it difficult for him to set aside resentments and bitterness. The Moon's subjective and instinctual emotional nature, however, is strengthened by being in sect. Dole's Jupiter, on the other hand, is out of sect and can lack the confidence and daring that challenging situations sometimes require. Dole appears by chart analysis not to be the "happy warrior" on the campaign trail.

Now view President Clinton's daytime chart where Mercury and Saturn — both diurnal planets — are on the same side of the horizon as the Sun. Thus, these planets are completely in sect. Anyone who has spent five minutes with Bill Clinton would never doubt he has a diurnal Mercury! Although his Saturn is in detriment in Leo, the planet is stronger by being in a strong house and strongly in sect.[8] In spite of his alleged inconsistency and lack of focus (which might be due to a Saturn in detriment), Clinton displays resiliency, tries hard to learn from his mistakes, and does not become discouraged. We'll talk more about diurnal Saturn below.

Also, note Clinton's Moon in Taurus, a nocturnal planet diurnally placed in a daytime chart. For an individual with the Moon in retentive Taurus, Clinton is emotionally expressive and self-revealing. It is not always clear (to this author, at least) what of Clinton's expression is display and what is genuine. These are characteristics of a Moon that is out of sect and heated up by the day.

Criterion #3: Is the Planet in a Masculine or Feminine Zodiacal Sign?

If a planet is in a masculine sign (fire or air triplicity), that planet has more diurnality; if a planet is in a feminine sign (earth or water triplicity), this increases its nocturnality. An exception, according to later classical astrology, is Mars, which is a nocturnal but masculine planet.

Bob Dole's Moon in Scorpio is therefore completely in sect (called *Hayz* by the Arabs and Medievals). Using all three criteria, the Moon is in a nighttime chart; clearly is nocturnal to the Sun by placement; and is in a feminine sign. On the other hand, Dole's Jupiter, a diurnal planet, is completely out of sect (called *Contrariety* of *Hayz* or *extra conditione*). Jupiter is a diurnal planet. Yet in Dole's nighttime chart Jupiter must function within a wholly nocturnal environment since he is nocturnally placed and in a feminine sign. Dole's Moon and Jupiter, both in Scorpio, only add to the nocturnal environment of these planets.

When we look at Clinton's chart, we see that both Mercury and Saturn are in Hayz. Mercury (before the Sun) and Saturn are diurnal planets; they are on the same side of the horizon as the Sun; and they are in masculine signs. Clinton's Moon, which is diurnally placed, is not completely out of sect because she's in earthy Taurus (and is in her exaltation there). Regardless of the 'Slick Willy' epithet people who meet him tend to connect with him emotionally. This might not be true if the Moon were in a fire or air sign, which would cause the Moon to be in Contrariety of Hayz.

This third criterion, sign placement by gender, strengthens Dole's Saturn and Clinton's Jupiter. Both planets are intrinsically diurnal and are in masculine Libra. The relative strengths of Dole's Saturn and Clinton's Jupiter obviously reflect in the styles and strengths of these two men. Dole was born at night but his Saturn, which is a diurnal planet, is on the same side of the horizon with the Sun and in masculine Libra. Dole is focused, self-disciplined, and responsible. In a nocturnal chart and with Saturn in the 6th House, Dole's Saturn has a melancholy side.

Clinton's Jupiter, a diurnal planet within a diurnal chart, is on the other side of the horizon as the Sun and, therefore, nocturnally placed. But Clinton's Jupiter has more diurnality because the planet is in the masculine sign of Libra.[9] Clinton seems to perform much better when he has a cause or can articulate a vision. He has also begun to enjoy "looking presidential," which means "being" Jupiter.

Now that you've worked with Clinton's and Dole's charts, take a look at your own chart. Planetary sect affects all seven classical planets. Whether you have a nighttime or a daytime chart, some of your planets are more in sect than others. (It is clearly impossible for all your planets to be in sect.) A planet can change its tone based on its relative diurnality or nocturnality.

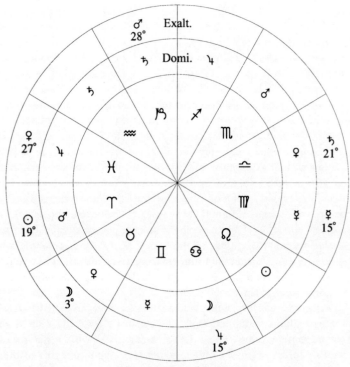

Figure 5.3 Wheel of Dignities

Note that the signs of detriment are opposite the signs of the planets' domicile ruler, and that the signs of fall are opposite the planets' exaltations.

Now I'd like to take a look at the seven classical planets according to diurnality or nocturnality. I'll begin with the most diurnal, the Sun, and end with the most nocturnal, the Moon. This causes us to take an important look at the signs of the zodiac. Each of the starry planets,

Mercury through Saturn, have two domicile rulers, one more diurnal and one more nocturnal. The two luminaries have one sign each in conformity with their sect (See Figure 5.3, which diagrams the planets' essential dignities by domicile and exaltation. For further detailed information on these essential dignities, see Chapter 1: "Dignity and Disposition in Ancient Astrology.")

Although modern astrologers use zodiacal signs in a more polished way than we find in classical astrology, there is much to learn from astrology's past about zodiacal position. Nowadays it is common to approach the signs of the zodiac through myth, legend, and psychological introspection. Here we will touch upon other avenues of access — through planetary rulership and triplicity (or element).

Planets and Signs

As the leader of the diurnal sect, the **Sun** is the most diurnal planet. The Sun's role in the chart is to radiate, to energize, and to show our joy in being alive. Diurnal conditions can enhance these factors. The Sun rules Leo, is exalted in Aries, and is the triplicity ruler of the fire triplicity by day. If the Sun is in essential dignity in a nocturnal chart, one can be confidently solar but may express this in a more subdued and introspective way. A nocturnal Sun on the whole may be less self-centered, more deliberative or reliable, and less radiant.

Note Bill Clinton's Leo Sun in a diurnal chart; contrast that with Bob Dole's Cancer Sun in a nocturnal chart, and watch how differently they present themselves in public! The Sun being in a daytime or nighttime chart, and in a masculine or feminine sign, will influence how he shines.

Now, you may say, "But Sun is in detriment in Aquarius and in fall in Libra, and these are both masculine signs." Aquarius and Libra are signs heavily disposed by Saturn, the Sun's intrinsic opposite. A Sun in these masculine signs in a daytime chart will bring out the diurnal nature of the chart but may be miscast, like Woody Allen in the title role of an otherwise well-done Batman movie.

Jupiter is the next most diurnal planet. He is domicile ruler of two signs, Sagittarius and Pisces, and is exalted in Cancer. Jupiter is the triplicity ruler of the fire triplicity at night. Jupiter is also the greater benefic and has a mostly positive influence in a birth chart. Clearly Jupiter has beneficial qualities either in a diurnal or nocturnal chart. According to Dorotheus, quoted in Hephaistio of Thebes,[10] Jupiter prefers Sagittarius most of all; this accords well with Jupiter's diurnality. Not unlike the Sun diurnal Jupiter is more robust, expansive, adventurous, and outgoing; a nocturnal Jupiter is quieter, more modest, more careful.

Interestingly, Jupiter has dignity in the water signs Pisces and Cancer, and is in debility in the earth signs Virgo (detriment) and Capricorn (fall). Remembering the dryness of the earth triplicity[11] this shows us that Jupiter cannot happily be boxed in by firm structures and too many rules. The water triplicity, however, brings out Jupiter's generosity and sensitivity. In Scorpio (note Dole's Jupiter) there is more parsimony — Scorpio is the driest sign of the water triplicity. (Compare Scorpio with the wetness of Pisces and Cancer, Humphrey Bogart with Charles Laughton!)

Saturn is the next diurnal planet. He is domicile ruler for Capricorn and Aquarius, is exalted in Libra, and is the triplicity ruler for the air signs by day.

Why, you may ask, is Saturn, of all planets, a diurnal planet? It is so for the same reason that Mars is a nocturnal planet — the influence of diurnality or nocturnality balances the potential excesses of these malefics.

Consider the difference between Saturn's two domicile signs, Capricorn and Aquarius. Would you rather have your Saturn in Aquarius or in Capricorn? Aquarius, a masculine sign, brings out a *diurnal Saturn* which is more outgoing and active without becoming depressive or oppressive. Aquarius is socially responsive and methodical but, as a sign of the air triplicity, is capable of elegance and objective analysis. A diurnal Saturn is organized and disciplined, but also responds to novelty and change. This Saturn creates and maintains new forms. Saturn, at his best, provides the virtues needed to flourish in a difficult world — self-discipline, self-reliance, consistency, responsibil-ity, and frugality. A diurnal Saturn provides these qualities, but with less dourness. I suspect that if Dole's Saturn were in a diurnal chart and a house more profitable than the 6th, his obvious Saturnine virtues would include more cheerfulness. Throughout his life Dole has bounced back from great difficulties, from war wounds to bitter political defeats.

Contrast this with *nocturnal Saturn*, the nocturnal ruler of the sign Capricorn. This placement is purely Saturnine in a serious authoritarian way. A nocturnal Saturn can become more melancholy, more prone to punishing oneself or others. Here gravity can become density and a greater sense of life's futility. Indeed, diurnality balances some of these Saturnine extremes!

Now we come to the planet that swings both ways, **Mercury.** In short a diurnal Mercury is more like the sign of his domicile rulership, Gemini, and a nocturnal Mercury more like the sign of his other domicile rulership, Virgo.

Mercury is not only communication and perception, but also intellect, our active abilities to make sense of our experience. Mercury is analytical as well as synthetic. He is strong both diurnally and nocturnally. Diurnal Mercury is clever, engaging, and spontaneous, compared with the more deliberate and quieter nocturnal Mercury. In Gemini Mercury can be clever but entirely too restless or scattered. Virgo's Mercury may be less dazzling but more capable of taking responsibility and solving practical problems. Both versions of Mercury are quite strong and competent. You might like the nocturnal Mercury in Virgo to organize your dinner party, but would prefer the diurnal Mercury in Gemini to attend.

Mercury appears to prefer slightly his nocturnal version. He is both domicile ruler and exaltation ruler in Virgo; He is also the triplicity ruler for the air signs in a nighttime chart. In his movement with the Sun Mercury (like Venus) emerges from the Sun's beams in direct motion when he is setting behind the Sun, and setting behind the Sun is a more nocturnal condition. These would slightly favor a nocturnal over a diurnal quality for Mercury.

The clever reader may now say, "But Mercury is in both detriment and fall in Pisces, and this is a nocturnal sign!" Mercury in sect and in Pisces can be supported by a nocturnal chart, but he may not be very Mercurial. Mercury requires form from which to organize and communicate his experience, and Pisces is the most formless of the zodiacal signs as the wettest sign of the water triplicity.

Now we move to the planets more intrinsically nocturnal than diurnal beginning with **Venus.** Is Venus a hot or a cold planet? The Greeks saw Venus as slightly warm and the Arabs and Medievals saw Venus as colder. Indeed, Venus, like music, "hath charms to soothe the savage breast," but also warms up the person burdened by the cares of life. Venus, therefore, has a moderating influence on a chart. Venus's nocturnality comes from her wetness — her ability to gather, attract, and create bonds.

The diurnal Venus is a more Libran Venus, and the nocturnal Venus more Taurean. The Libran Venus is socially responsive, affable, and motivated by beauty; but is somewhat impersonal, and yet tries too hard. (Ask Bill Clinton!) The Taurean Venus soothes, attracts, and is sensual. Venus's detriment in nocturnal Scorpio shows the contradiction between the desires for happiness and pleasure and those for intense emotional experience. Venus is exalted in Pisces and has her fall in Virgo — she flourishes in a moist zodiacal environment. On the other hand, Scorpio is the driest sign of the water triplicity.

Next in nocturnality is **Mars.** According to Ptolemy the ancients apportioned dry Mars to the moisture of the night.[12] There is an interesting distinction between how the Greek and the Arab and Medieval traditions handled the zodiacal status of Mars in sect. I shall begin with the Greeks. Both traditions in assessing Mars's dignity follow Ptolemy's triplicity rulers and give Mars as the triplicity ruler for the water signs day and night.[13] The moisture of night allows Mars personal connection and sensitivity. Indeed, Mars can be most difficult when impersonal and unconcerned for others.

Think of the difference between Mars in his two domicile rulerships, masculine (fiery) Aries and feminine (watery) Scorpio. Mars is happily himself in Aries but this diurnal sign can make Mars more impulsive and combative. This can be very helpful when one's safety is threatened, or when arguing on some talk radio program, but less helpful when negotiating with a traffic cop or one's boss. In Scorpio Mars is less noisy, in better contact with his vulnerabilities, and moves his energy directly toward his purpose. For the Arabs and for later astrologers Mars prefers a diurnal sign because of his inherent masculine nature. If you make Mars too moist, you get too many "sensitive New Age guys." The Arab and Medieval traditions would have none of that.

Looking at the signs of Mars's detriment and fall, Taurus (along with Libra) and Cancer, respectively, it seems that the later Arab and Medieval traditions are correct, as both Taurus and Cancer are nocturnal signs. On the other hand, Taurus is slow considering Mars's need for a free range of motion, and Cancer as the most personal sign of the water triplicity may shy away from the good fight.

I tend to side with the Greek tradition, although I invite my fellow astrologers to try out both alternatives. As Rob Hand has said, the later traditions may have confused sect with sex.[14] All traditions are consistent, however, that Mars is in sect in a nocturnal chart, with the Sun below the horizon.

This brings us to the most nocturnal planet, the nocturnal sect-leader, the **Moon.** The Moon's nocturnality is a function of her moisture, not her coolness. The fully nocturnal Moon is sensitive, caring, and emotionally strong. A diurnal Moon is a Moon out of sect — her intrinsic nocturnality is not appreciated by the chart's diurnal environment. Bill Clinton has given us a hint. The diurnal Moon can be restless, over-eager, and perhaps have greater expressiveness than internal wisdom.

A strong Moon especially enhanced by being in sect in a chart can cause a person to be emotionally and instinctively in touch, and may be an important ingredient for success in life. As the Moon is (and has always been) the maternal stellar body, I am reminded of a famous quote by Sigmund Freud, "A man who has been the indisputable favorite of his mother keeps for life the feeling of a conqueror, that confidence of success that often induces real success."[15]

Here I conclude an initial look at the important issue of planetary sect in astrology. As a perusal of Dole's and Clinton's charts shows, planetary sect is not a quaint relic of an astrology long-forgotten but provides new possibilities for chart comprehension and analysis. I invite you to continue working with your chart and those of others to gain a greater appreciation of the legacy of ancient astrology.

References and Notes

1. For a more complete account of planetary sect see Robert Hand, *Night and Day: Planetary Sect in Astrology,* (Berkeley Springs, WV: ARHAT, 1995).
2. Ptolemy, *Tetrabiblos, Book I*, R. Schmidt, trans., (Berkeley Springs, WV: Golden Hind Press, 1994).
3. Bill Clinton, August 19, 1946; 8:51 a.m. CST, Hope, Arkansas. Birth data from mother in a 1992 personal communication with Lois Rodden. Bob Dole, July 22, 1923; 12:10 a.m. CST; Russell, Kansas. Birth data from Joylynn Hill, *Mercury Hour,* 1/77. Recently, however, a different time for Dole has emerged, from an autobiography written in 1988 (from Lois Rodden's *Data News #58*, March 1996). Lois Rodden has made attempts to contact Dole's office for clarification, with no response as yet. (Personal communication, 6/16/96.)
4. *Tetrabiblos I,* Ch 7, p. 18.
5. This classical distinction of elements and qualities is important to later medical and psychological astrology through the Renaissance. Importantly, Ptolemy discusses the four qualities extensively in *Tetrabiblos* but does not relate these qualities to planets. In Vettius Valens' *The Anthology, Book I*, written in 2nd century C.E. (R. Schmidt, trans.,) Valens relates the signs to the four elements. So far, Valens' work is the first evidence of this tradition.
6. Antiochus of Athens, *The Thesaurus*, R. Schmidt, trans., (Berkeley Springs, WV: Golden Hind Press, 1993), Chapter 44.
7. Vettius Valens, *The Anthology, Book III*, R. Schmidt, trans., (Berkeley Springs, WV: Golden Hind Press, 1994), Ch 6..
8. Diurnal Mercury and Saturn, preceding the Sun, are the Sun's "spear bearers." According to Ptolemy's *Tetrabiblos, Book IV*, Chapter 3, this is quite fortunate for rank and prestige.

9.Clinton's Jupiter is also conjunct the benefic fixed star Spica. According to Robson, Spica with Jupiter manifests as "popular, social success, wealth, ecclesiastical honor, and preferment." *Fixed Stars and Constellations in Astrology,* (Bombay, India: Taraporevala, 1987) 212.

10. Hephaistio of Thebes, *Apotelesmatics, Book I*, R. Schmidt, trans., (Berkeley Springs, WV: Golden Hind Press, 1994).

11. Using Aristotelian qualities, earth is cold and dry; using Stoic qualities, earth is only dry. For the more common Aristotelian version of the elements, see, for example, Lilly's *Christian Astrology, 533 -4*, (1985 Regulus Reprint). Earlier references are in Ramon Lull, Guido Bonatti, and the Renaissance Johannes Schoener.

12. *Ibid.,* Ch 7.

13. There is another form of triplicity rulers, attributed to Dorotheus of Sidon in the 1st century C.E., which gives three planets instead of two to the four triplicities. In this system, Venus is the triplicity ruler of the Water triplicity by day, Mars by night. This system seems used more for disposition than dignity.

14. Robert Hand, *Night and Day*, 6.

15. Ernest Jones, *The Life and Work of Sigmund Freud,* abridgment by Lionel Trilling, (New York: Basic Books, 1961), 6.

Chapter 6: The Phases of the Planets

This section examines how planets change in strength and meaning according to their phase with the Sun. A planet's phase relationship to the Sun determines the planet's direction (direct or retrograde), its speed, and, most importantly, how and when it appears in the sky.

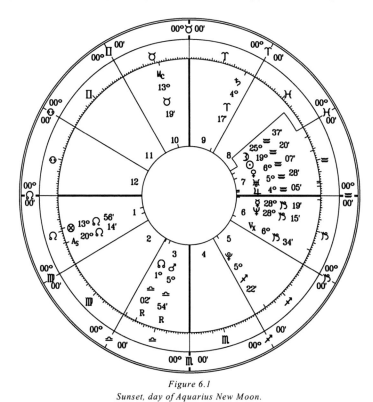

Figure 6.1
Sunset, day of Aquarius New Moon.

The Moon is too close to the Sun for us to see her. She is quickly moving away from the Sun.

Although this is an important feature of ancient and medieval astrological analysis, only a shadow of it survives into modern astrology.[1] The factors accounting for this loss are that we are now less aware of planets as they appear in the sky and the astrological tradition itself is complex. There are many issues to disentangle, and for that purpose we will examine Hellenistic Greek astrology and medieval astrology.

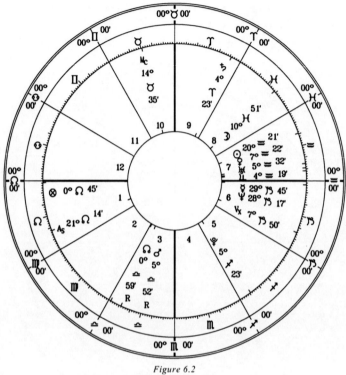

Figure 6.2
Sunset, day after New Moon

The Moon, moving ahead of the Sun in the zodiac, rises from the Sun's beams, appearing as a thin crescent at sunset.

Diurnal and Zodiacal Motion Together

To begin, we must become comfortable with integrating the planets' two motions — their zodiacal motion, which is *counterclockwise,* and their diurnal motion, which is *clockwise.* While modern astrology stresses a planet's counterclockwise motion through the zodiac, the planets also move clockwise according to the apparent daily rotation of the sky. Although the planets move at varying speeds through the zodiac, each and every day the Sun, Moon, and planets rise above the eastern horizon, culminate at the Midheaven, set at the Descendant, and anticulminate at the I.C.

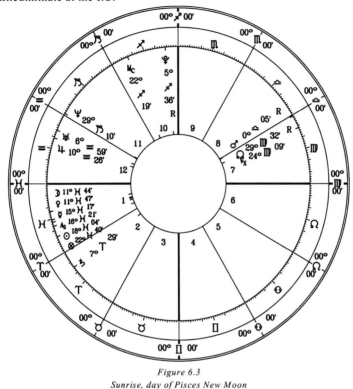

Figure 6.3
Sunrise, day of Pisces New Moon

The Moon is moving toward the Sun. The last time we'll see her is just before sunrise.

To bring these two motions together let's examine the phases of the Moon for February and March 1997. At sunset on the day of the Aquarius New Moon (February 7) the Sun and Moon are so close together that we cannot see the Moon. (See Figure 6.1) Once the Moon separates from the Sun moving counterclockwise through the zodiac, we can see the Moon as a thin crescent that appears at sunset. Moving in a clockwise direction the Sun will set before the Moon. When the crescent Moon first becomes visible after the New Moon, she is **heliacally rising,** rising *from the Sun.* The next day at sunset the Moon is 12° further from the Sun in the zodiac, and thus is larger and higher in the sky. (See Figure 6.2) This continues for the next twelve or thirteen days until the Moon becomes full, when the Moon rises as the Sun is setting. Then, as she begins to wane, the Moon rises later each night becoming smaller and smaller as she moves about 12° closer to the Sun each day until the Moon is but a thin sliver that is visible just before dawn. At the end of the cycle when we see the Moon for the last time in the predawn hours before she moves too close to the Sun to be seen, the Moon's condition is **heliacally setting** because she is setting *into the Sun.* (See Figure 6.3)

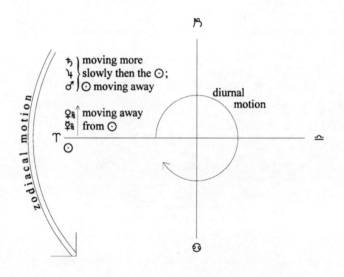

Figure 6.4
Heliacally Rising in the East

All planets rise and set each day on the horizon, reflecting the sky's apparent rotation. Yet they are also heliacally rising and setting but not each day. Instead, heliacal risings and settings are determined by planetary motions that take place over a much longer period of time than the risings and settings of their diurnal clockwise motion. In addition, while planets can only rise in the east and only set in the west, they can heliacally rise and set both in the east and in the west!

Heliacally Rising and Setting in the East

There are two conditions for heliacally rising in the east, which is when a planet makes its first appearance from the Sun before dawn. The first condition involves the "superior" planets — Mars, Jupiter, Saturn — which because of their natural speeds move more slowly than the Sun. Since the Sun moves through the zodiac faster than these planets, during his yearly orbit the Sun will conjoin each of them then separate from them in a counterclockwise motion. When the separation is around 15° or 17°, we can see that planet rising in the east before the Sun rises in the morning.[2] Therefore, each one is heliacally rising. (See Figure 6.4.)

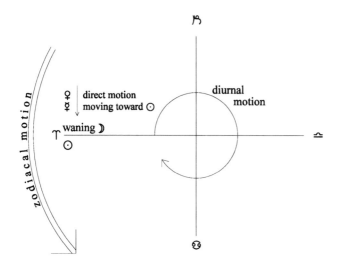

Figure 6.5
Heliacally Setting in the East

The second condition is when the "inferior" planets, Mercury and

Venus, are *retrograde*. When Venus or Mars are retrograde, they move in a direction opposite from the Sun. After Mercury or Venus makes a retrograde conjunction with the Sun (their "inferior conjunction"), and the Sun moves sufficiently ahead of Mercury or Venus in the zodiac, one can see Mercury or Venus before the Sun rises. When any of the classical planets (except the Moon which can't do this) rise before the Sun in the east, we call them each "morning stars."

Likewise, a planet heliacally *sets* in the east when the planet moves faster than the Sun and moves into the light. This happens when Mercury and Venus have gone direct in motion and are moving very quickly. Also after she enters her waning crescent phase, the Moon sets in the east. *(See Figure 6.5)*

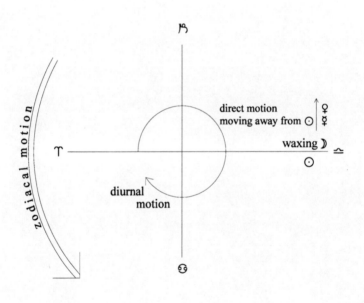

Figure 6.6
Heliacally Rising in the West

When a planet moves *faster* in direct motion than the Sun, it heliacally rises in the west appearing at sunset. When Mercury or Venus have had their direct conjunctions with the Sun (the "superior conjunctions"), they move at their fastest speeds. Moving ahead of the Sun in the zodiac, Mercury or Venus now become visible as "evening stars" as the Sun is setting. Picture the Sun just down under the horizon, with Mercury and Venus direct and far enough ahead of the Sun, becoming visible in the west above the horizon. We see them as they are heliacally rising. (See Figure 6.6) The Moon, as stated previously, heliacally rises (first appears from the Sun) only in the west after sunset, and heliacally sets (last appears) in the east.

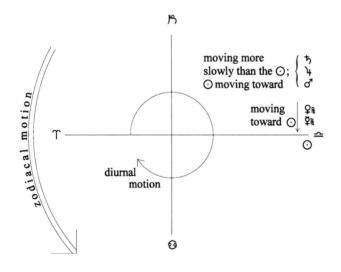

Figure 6.7
Heliacally Setting in the West

All planets (except the Moon) can heliacally set in the west, disappearing into the Sun's beams after last being seen in the evening after sunset. This occurs when Mercury and Venus become retrograde and the Sun moves close to them, and when the faster-moving Sun closes in on Mars, Jupiter, and Saturn before their respective conjunctions with the Sun. (See Figure 6.7.)

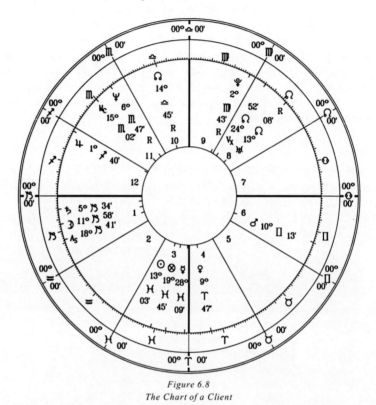

Figure 6.8
The Chart of a Client

Although Mercury and Venus are in signs of detriment, look again! Mercury is just emerging from the Sun's beams, and Venus is continuing to rise ahead of the Sun so that in the west it moves further away from it and becomes brighter. They are both strong in the chart, to which my client, who is an artist and student astrologer, can attest.

*Note that Saturn is rising ahead of the Sun in the east and Mars is moving closer to the Sun because the Sun is a faster planet.

Traditionally heliacal rising and setting were major factors in chart delineation showing a planet's strength or weakness. A planet rising from the Sun (in either the east or the west) is like a warrior coming out of a battle victorious (Bonatti),[3] or a planet recovering from a sickness and being restored to health (Al-Biruni).[4] A planet's condition of heliacally rising may compensate for other difficulties such as being in a sign of detriment. (See Figure 6.8.) A planet going into the Sun's beams (between 12° and 15° away from the Sun and moving closer) is moving into debility. Moving into the beams may decrease the potency of a planet that is otherwise well situated. For interpretative purposes we may consider a heliacally rising planet as if it were in the 1st or 10th House, a heliacally setting planet as if is moving toward a 12th-house placement, and a planet within the Sun's beams as if were in the 12th House. (Mercury, which is mostly under the Sun's beams, may be an exception.)

Oriental and Occidental

The words *oriental* and *occidental* also refer to a planet's phase with the Sun. Yet astrology's traditions have not used these words consistently. In modern English *oriental* has become another word for "East" and *occidental* another word for "West." Yet, the Greek, Latin, and Arabic words for oriental and occidental also mean heliacal rising and setting.

As we have seen, not all planets heliacally rise (first appear) from the Sun in the east, but only those that are moving more slowly than the Sun — Mars, Jupiter, Saturn, and retrograde Mercury and Venus as the morning stars. The Moon and direct Mercury and Venus, moving faster than the Sun, can all rise in the west! Furthermore, when a planet does rise in the east, orientally, it is not that the planet is east of the Sun but that *the Sun is east of the planet!* Remember that at sunrise the Sun is east on the horizon and the oriental planet is west of the Sun. On the other hand, an occidental planet is east of the Sun, since at sunset the *Sun is west of the planet.* It might be clearer to call a planet oriental if it heliacally rises (first appears from the Sun) in the east or west, and occidental if it heliacally sets (last appears) in the east or west. But alas, astrology's traditions are not consistent.

The medieval tradition has the advantage of utter simplicity. (See Figure 6.9) Astrologers called the superior planets Mars, Jupiter, and Saturn, oriental from the conjunction of the Sun to their opposition, and occidental from the time of the opposition back to the conjunction.[5]

As morning stars Venus and Mercury are oriental (the Sun is east of them), and as evening stars they are occidental (the Sun is west of them, having set before them). The medieval tradition subsumes the occidental and oriental Moon into her waxing and waning qualities, respectively.[6] Dividing the sky into oriental and occidental halves differs from the Hellenistic Greek use of oriental and occidental quadrants. What accounts for the medieval view? In *On the Judgment of Nativities* 14th-Century astrologer Antonio de Montulmo brings together a planet being oriental "to the Sun," "to the Ascendant," and being above the horizon.[7] Why does Montulmo do this? If a planet is oriental and if you place the Sun at the Ascendant (as he is at sunrise), that planet is *always* above the horizon, *always* in the day half of the map of the heavens. If a planet is occidental, from the opposition back to the conjunction, it *always* appears in the sky behind the Sun at sunset.[8] This system renders orientality diurnal (and masculine) in nature, while occidentality is nocturnal (and feminine) in nature.

Minor Accidental Dignities and Debilities

Medieval astrology uses conditions of oriental and occidental as *minor accidental dignities* for the planets. According to Lilly's tabulation of accidental dignities and debilities in *Christian Astrology* Mars, Jupiter, and Saturn receive two points when oriental (from conjunction to opposition) and lose two points when occidental (from opposition to conjunction). Mercury and Venus, however, gain two points when occidental (in the evening sky), and lose two points when oriental (in the predawn sky).[9]

Why are Mercury and Venus "better" when occidental? When Mercury and Venus appear at sunset and are heliacally rising, they are in direct motion. (See Figure 6.6.) When they appear before sunrise and are heliacally rising, they are retrograde. Thus, Mercury and Venus are better when occidental because they are both heliacally rising and moving in direct motion. (The Moon is also stronger when waxing and occidental, weaker when waning and oriental.)

The Greek tradition does not use orientality and occidentality as minor strengths or weaknesses of a planet but rather appears to have used oriental and occidental in a descriptive way, as we shall see.

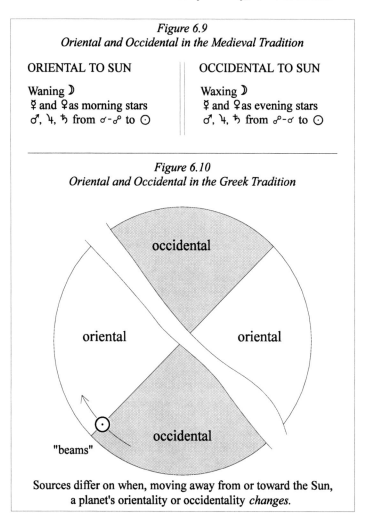

Figure 6.9
Oriental and Occidental in the Medieval Tradition

ORIENTAL TO SUN	OCCIDENTAL TO SUN
Waning ☽	Waxing ☽
☿ and ♀ as morning stars	☿ and ♀ as evening stars
♂, ♃, ♄ from ☌-☍ to ☉	♂, ♃, ♄ from ☍-☌ to ☉

Figure 6.10
Oriental and Occidental in the Greek Tradition

occidental

oriental   oriental

occidental

"beams"

Sources differ on when, moving away from or toward the Sun, a planet's orientality or occidentality *changes*.

Young and Old, Early and Late

When the Sun rises in the east, the day is young, and what rises before the Sun also rises earlier than the Sun. After the Sun sets in the west, what follows the Sun and sets after the Sun is later. This simple observation of the heavens furnishes a wealth of interpretative material.

The distinction of oriental as being early or young, occidental as being late or old, survives well into the 17th Century. William Lilly uses the young/old and early/late in horary and natal analysis. In a question about property an oriental significator means "the trees are young ones or wood of small growth," and if the significator is occidental, the wood is ancient and of more growth.[10] In determining the age of a thief an oriental significator is young, an occidental significator is old.[11] In a question about sickness an oriental significator denotes a new sickness, whereas an occidental significator denotes a chronic one.[12]

In his natal analysis Lilly gives us the following formula to answer the question: "About what part of life or when the native may expect Wealth or the Goods of Fortune?" If the significators of wealth in a birth chart are oriental of the Sun, wealth arrives early; if occidental, wealth arrives late.[13]

Temperament and Complexion

By "temperament" I mean the form of the body and what we might call one's basic "energy." The astrologer assesses planets for polarities of hot and cold (high-spirited or more sedate), and moist and dry (fleshier or thinner, more emotional or more cerebral) to come up with a mixture, what is called a "complexion." One determines whether sanguine (hot and moist), choleric (hot and dry), melancholic (cold and dry), or phlegmatic (cold and moist) predominates. To determine temperament and body shape one "collects testimonies" from planets in the 1st House, planets aspecting the Ascendant, and planets ruling the Ascendant.[14] It is not a planet's element or sign placement that is important, buts its orientality or occidentality. (One adds qualities for the sign of the Ascendant, the phase of the Moon, and the season of the Sun.)

Oriental gives a larger frame, more activity, and curly hair; occidental more moderate or shorter stature, thinner build, and straighter hair. Modern readers are more likely to think psychologically, and astrological tradition certainly provides room for that. Although a "fleshy body" can mean one that's overweight, a "moist" person is also quieter or less frenetic. Try these out on yourself and your friends!

Earlier in the *Tetrabiblos,* Ptolemy states that **Saturn** naturally cools and slightly dries.[15] Saturn, when oriental, is cold and moist, but when occidental he is dry. Oriental Saturn, if he is the significator of the body, is more robust, gives moderate stature, and curly hair; when occidental, Saturn is darker, gives a leaner build, with hair that is black, straight, or sparse.

Jupiter is hot and moist when oriental, as is his intrinsic nature. When occidental, he remains moist. His relation with the Sun does not substantially alter Jupiter's basic nature. More specifically, oriental Jupiter makes for good stature, lighter skin, and "intermediate hair" (between straight and curly). An occidental Jupiter gives less hair, straighter hair, and leans more to the wet (fleshy).

Mars has a "nature chiefly to dry and to burn," according to Ptolemy.[16] When oriental, Mars has both qualities. Being occidental accentuates Mars's dryness. When Mars is a significator of the body and is oriental, Mars is robust, gives a large stature, a whitish-red complexion with light blue eyes, and shaggy or medium hair. When occidental, Mars gives a body more medium in stature, more red in the skin, with smooth hair or less hair.

Venus is hot and moist when oriental, yet only moist when occidental. The moisture of Venus is her predominant quality, and this doesn't change. Whether oriental or occidental, Venus gives many of the same physical characteristics as Jupiter although Venus is more "feminine" more shapely and graceful, more delicate and more plump — "and on its own [Venus] makes the eyes blue with comeliness."[17]

Mercury is hot when oriental, dry when occidental. A body signified by an oriental Mercury is medium in stature, graceful, with small body and intermediate hair. When occidental, the body is lean and slender, the hair smoother or more reddish.

How do the **Sun** and **Moon** weigh in? When aspecting, ruling, or on the Ascendant, the *Sun* gives greater size and robustness (Sun is hot and dry by nature but less so than Mars). The *Moon* makes one more moderate in stature and adds moisture.

What are the effects of a planet's orientality and occidentality on body type and temperament? Except for Saturn, being oriental heats up the planets; being occidental maintains the moisture of the benefics, Jupiter and Venus, but dries out the others. In general, oriental is hotter and wetter, and occidental is colder and drier.

Significant planets which are oriental give physical qualities that are *more youthful,* these being moisture and heat; occidental planets give greater dryness and reduce heat, which is a condition of *becoming older.* Jupiter and Venus, the two benefics, which retain moisture even when occidental, are moderate and life-preserving.[18]

Does this mean that a person with occidental significators is born with an old body? Think of it in this way: an older person is usually thinner (drier) and less energetic (colder). A person with an excess of cold and dry may be more awkward as a child and young person, more comfortable as an older adult. Conversely, a person with oriental significators of body is more energetic and fleshier, but may not age as comfortably.

Other testimonies of quality also concern this distinction of young and old. The waxing Moon's phase promotes moisture, then heat, and dryness and coldness when waning. The Sun's quarters beginning with the winter solstice (not the spring equinox), first increases moisture, then heat, then dryness, then coldness.

Oriental and Occidental Quadrants: The Greek Tradition

There is no evidence that the Greek tradition thought a planet oriental from the conjunction to the opposition, and occidental from the opposition back to the conjunction. The ancients used not halves but quadrants. What are oriental and occidental *quadrants?* I quote Ptolemy, from *Book III*, Chapter 3, of *Tetrabiblos.*

> For the general time of the effect, it is necessary to examine whether they are East or West relative to the Sun and the *Horoskopos, the quadrants preceding each of them and their diameters being East, while the remaining quadrants are West* [emphasis mine], also, whether they should happen to be upon the pivot points or post-ascensions. For when they are East or upon a pivot, they become more effective at the commencement, while when they are West and upon the post-ascension, they are tardy."[19]

Ptolemy, as do others, correlates configurations to the Ascendant (rising above the horizon, culminating, setting, and anticulminating) with phases with the Sun.

Ascendant and Solar Quadrants

In the configurations *to the Ascendant,* the oriental quadrants are between rising and culminating and between setting and anticulminating. The occidental quarters are between culminating and setting and between anticulminating and rising. Both Medieval and Greek astrologers agree on this point. Using a quadrant house system, where the 1st-House cusp is the Ascendant and the 10th-House cusp is the Midheaven, the oriental quadrants are Houses 10-12 and 4-6; the occidental quadrants are Houses 7-9 and 1-3. (See Figure 6.10)

Oriental and occidental quadrants from the Ascendant denote masculine and feminine. The Greek tradition holds that oriental quadrants are masculine, and occidental quadrants are feminine. Delineating masculine and feminine quadrants survives later in this form.

Why are the oriental quadrants masculine, and the occidental ones feminine? Oriental quadrants precede the Sun at sunrise and at sunset, when the day and night change into the other. A planet in Houses 10-12 and 4-6, in oriental and masculine quadrants, will *both* be in the eastern side of the sky at sunrise or at sunset. The Sun ascends in the eastern half of the sky, and is more masculine; the Sun descends in the western half of the sky, and is more feminine.

The question arises *how could you use oriental and occidental quadrants to the Sun?* How do we divide the two halves of the cycle from the conjunction to the opposition, and from the opposition back to the conjunction *each* of which has an oriental and an occidental section?

One possibility follows the diurnal cycle and the Ascendant quadrants. Take a chart and turn it backward and forward to the sunrise and sunset of that day. All planets that are above the horizon in the east at sunrise or sunset are oriental; all planets that are above the horizon in the west at sunrise or sunset are occidental. These do not give easy 90° separations between zones of oriental and occidental because the distance between horizon and Midheaven changes during the day. At higher northern or southern latitudes the distances change dramatically. Although difficult in practice this alternative may be closer to the ancient approach.

Another way is to follow a pattern similar to the Moon's quarters. From the Sun the first 90° is oriental, and to the opposition at 180° is occidental. From the opposition the following 90° is oriental, and the last 90° back to the Sun is occidental. There is justification for this simpler approach because in assessing temperament, one uses the Moon's phases in addition to a planet's orientality and occidentality.

Complete Phases of Planets with the Sun

At the beginning of this chapter I spoke of superior and inferior planets as they heliacally rise and set. I need to describe what happens *between* a planet heliacally rising (first appearance from the Sun) and heliacally setting (final appearance from the Sun).

The superior planets — Mars, Jupiter, and Saturn — quickly rise from the Sun's beams in the east. As the Sun continues to move away from these planets to about 60° from them, the planets become slower in motion. By the time the Sun is 90° away they appear to slow down abruptly. At about 120° they stop completely and appear to change direction, becoming retrograde. The Sun moving to their other side goes into opposition to these retrograde planets. At this time these planet rise as the Sun sets, similar to a Full Moon. This "acronycal rising" of a planet (when the planet rises as the Sun sets) completes the first half of the cycle. After the opposition the Sun begins to move closer to these planets, until, at about 120°, they again stop on their way toward becoming direct. Gradually these planets gain speed as the Sun moves closer to them, and eventually the superior planets set into the Sun's beams.

Al-Biruni from the 11th Century gives psychological metaphors for a superior planet in these phases. As mentioned before a planet rising from the Sun's beams is like a person recovering to strength after a long illness.

> The planet at its first resting place [stationary retrograde] appears strangled, hopeless, in the first section of the retrograde course sluggish and depressed, while in the second section [after the Sun's opposition] hope of succour is given, which is confirmed in the second station, delivery being at hand, while the direct course indicates, as its name suggests, prosperity and power.[20]

The inferior planets, Mercury and Venus, heliacally rise in their direct motion in the west, as they move faster than the Sun and appear in the evening. After Mercury and Venus come to maximum elongation, they begin to move slower and the Sun moves closer to them. When the Sun is about 20° away from Mercury and about 30° away from Venus, these planets stop and change direction to retrograde. Mercury and Venus then make their retrograde conjunction with the Sun, and then move onto the other side, rising heliacally in the east. After their direct stations, Mercury and Venus gain speed and move toward the slower Sun. At 15° to 17°, the inferior planets move into the Sun's beams, thereby heliacally setting in the east.

Qualities and Phases

Earlier we worked with the qualities of hot, cold, wet, and dry to determine the figure of the body and a person's temperament. We saw that the Moon's phases increase qualities of moisture, heat, dryness, then cold, respectively. The Sun's quarters, beginning with the winter solstice, follow the same pattern.

In Chapter 8 of *Tetrabiblos I*, Ptolemy divides the phases of the planets into sequences of the qualities. Beginning with heliacal rising to first station, a planet increases in moisture. From the first station to a planet's acronycal rising (rising in the east when the Sun sets), a planet increases in heat. From the acronycal rising to the direct station, a planet increases in dryness, and to the setting within the Sun's beams, a planet increases in coldness.

Oriental, Occidental, Retrograde, Under the Beams

Elsewhere in the literature we find complex descriptions of the phases of planets with the Sun. Al-Biruni and Paulus Alexandrinus (whose works are separated by seven centuries) both describe transitions of orientality and occidentality. Guido Bonatti in the 13th Century combines orientality and occidentality and a planet's gradations of strength and weakness.

According to Bonatti[21] when a superior planet emerges from the rays of the Sun, the planet becomes strong (it recovers from sickness) at 30°. When 60° away from the Sun, a planet is then "oriental going toward debility." (Notice that the planet is slowing down at this time.) At 90° it is "oriental and weak," (it is much slower), then "oriental retrograde." After the Sun's opposition until the planet goes direct, this planet is "occidental retrograde." A planet becomes stronger at its direct station, and much stronger at 60° from the Sun (it is beginning to go much faster). When the Sun has moved to within 30° of the planet, however, that planet is "occidental going toward debility." The debility is, of course, the heliacal setting when a planet is about 17° from the Sun with the Sun moving toward it.

Mercury and Venus follow a similar pattern. (According to Bonatti's tradition, Mercury and Venus are stronger when heliacally rising in the evening, when direct in motion, than in the morning.) When heliacally rising in the east, appearing as morning stars, they are "oriental and weak," because they are retrograde at this time. When Mercury and Venus are direct, until the point at which they are furthest away from the Sun, as when they go retrograde, they are "oriental and strong." They weaken as they hurl themselves into the Sun's beams. After the conjunction they soon move past the Sun becoming "occidental toward appearing." After heliacally rising in the west they are "occidental and strong" but 15° later they move toward debility and are slowing down. The retrograde station is the beginning of "occidental and weak." When Mercury and Venus go into the Sun's beams retrograde, they are "occidental retrograde and most debilitated." After the conjunction with the Sun they emerge ahead of the Sun in the morning and the process begins again.

Al-Biruni has a 30° and a 90° rule. A planet is strongly oriental only from heliacal rising (first appearance) until 30° from the Sun. "The term orientality ceases to be applicable" when a superior planet is 90° from the Sun, a point where the planet slows down considerably. Only when a planet, after its direct station, is 90° from the Sun (the Sun moving toward it), does its occidental phase begin.[22] A planet is strongly occidental only when 30° away from the Sun until the planet sets into the Sun's beams, having made its final appearance. In a planet's movement, its phases with the Sun, there are intermediate stages in which one should not use the expressions "oriental" and "occidental."

Paulus Alexandrinus, a Greek astrologer later than Ptolemy, and strongly influenced by him, wrote that stars have "dealings in the morning" until they form a right-hand triangle with the Sun; they "maintain their regard in the evening" when they are behind the Sun (in the zodiac, setting behind the Sun) up to a left-sided triangle. It is just beyond this distance from the Sun, 120°, that Mars, Jupiter, and Saturn turn retrograde; and when the Sun reaches the same distance on the other side, these planets go direct.[23]

Paulus's 120° is also the largest distance between the Ascendant and Midheaven degrees, and between the Descendant and Anticulminating degrees, at the latitude which the Ancients believed was the highest inhabitable latitude (about 49°).[24] (This occurs when the Ascendant is near 0° Cancer.) Here may be another parallel between a planet's configuration to the Sun and to the Ascendant.

For Paulus and Al-Biruni a planet may be *neither* oriental nor occidental at this point; they are simply retrograde or under the beams. When heliacally setting and "retracing their path," Paulus says a planet's productions are "ineffectual, unavailing, and insignificant."[25] Oriental and occidental, "morning" and "evening" planets, can be significant and effective, but not if those planets are heliacally setting, within the Sun's beams, or retrograde. Paulus and Al-Biruni only differ in the length of the oriental or morning phases, and the length of the occidental or evening phases. Al-Biruni uses 90°, similar to the quarters of the Moon;

Paulus uses 120°, the approximate distance from the Sun to a superior planet's direct and retrograde stations.

Phases with the Sun and Significations for the Soul

Here's another analysis of quadrant phases of planets with the Sun. Ptolemy, in *Book III* of the *Tetrabiblos,* and Antonio de Montulmo, in *On the Judgment of Nativities,* Part 2, both discuss the natures of the soul (psyche or personality) as determined from the birth chart. We are concerned with the *turning points* of the sequence.

What planet or planets are significant for the soul? Ptolemy gives a simple technique, examining planets that have the most dignities over the positions of the Moon and Ascendant. Ptolemy writes of two kinds of soul, the irrational (Moon) and the rational (Mercury). Ptolemy will find one planet that is the significator for the soul. (See also Chapter 4, page 65.)

Antonio de Montulmo, more Aristotelian in this matter than Ptolemy, distinguishes between vegetative or bodily soul, sensitive soul, and intellectual soul. Stating Montulmo's ideas far too simply, the Ascendant and 1st House signify the bodily soul; the Moon, the sensitive soul; and Mercury, the intellectual soul. Is there a planet that strongly predominates these positions in rulership? Is there a conflict between one planetary ruler and another? Which planet is stronger, which shows difficulties?

For both authors (Montulmo clearly following Ptolemy), how a planet configures with the Sun is another factor for describing the qualities of soul.

○ Ptolemy and Montulmo liken a superior planet on the Ascendant, if it is the significator, with one oriental — heliacally rising in the east. This planet, if it has rulership over the significators of the soul, "make souls liberal and simple and self-willed and strong and adept and keen and guileless."[26]

○ A planet at its retrograde (morning) station is like a planet on the Midheaven, and that planet is more steady, deliberate, practical, and of good understanding and memory.

○ A planet at (retrograde) opposition to the Sun is like a planet setting in the west, at the Descendant of a birth chart. It is weaker, more vacillating, fickle, and of a lower vitality.

o   A significant planet at the direct station is like a planet on the I.C., showing a less active mind but one that is interested in investigating the unseen and unknown through astrology, dream interpretation, and the like.

What if Mercury or Venus signifies soul? What is the influence of the inferior planets and their configurations with the Sun? Ptolemy gives us not a sentence, but *part* of a sentence! When he discusses a superior planet at I.C. or anticulmination, he mentions Mercury and Venus in this way: "furthermore, for Hermes and Aphrodite, the evening settings by day and the morning settings by night."[27] Therefore, it is not thoroughly explained by Ptolemy, and Montulmo gives us essentially the same lack of information.

What does this phrase "evening settings by day and morning settings by night" mean? It does *not* appear to refer to heliacal setting by day or night. This phrase seems to speak of west of the Sun, or occidental, in a daytime chart, and east of the Sun, or oriental, in a nighttime chart.

The conclusion is this. Within a diurnal chart the inferior cycle begins at the *morning rising*, heliacally rising retrograde in the east. For an evening chart, the inferior cycle begins at the *evening rising,* the heliacal rising direct in the west.

It appears that the Greek tradition, at least articulated by Ptolemy, may consider Mercury or Venus rising in the east, *in a morning chart,* (*i.e.,* just before dawn) more favorable even if that planet is retrograde. Conversely, Mercury or Venus heliacally rising in the west, in *an evening chart,* (*i.e.,* just after sunset) is favorable. In a diurnal chart Mercury and Venus heliacally rising in the east would be as if they were on the Ascendant, and the same for these planets heliacally rising in the west in a nighttime chart. We return to planetary sect, a unifying factor in Hellenistic Greek astrology. The reader may recall that as a morning star Mercury is judged diurnal, and as an evening star he is judged nocturnal. Much research and application remain.

References and Notes

1. Dane Rudhyar is one modern astrologer who stressed the "orbits" of the planets in relationship to the Sun. This is contained in material on "Parts of Planets" in *The Astrology of Personality* (first published in 1936 and available from Aurora Press), the cycles of the Moon and the Lot of Fortune in *The Lunation Cycle* (Aurora Press, 1967), and the cycles of Mercury and Venus in *An Astrological Study of Psychological Complexes* (Shambhala, 1976). Although Rudhyar does not identify his sources from astrology's history, this chapter makes clear how

indebted Rudhyar was to Claudius Ptolemy.

2. Due in part to differences in latitude, it is not easy to determine exactly when a planet becomes visible. Rising times from the Sun are connected with a planet's orb of aspect, from which we get aspect orb.

3. Bonatti, *Liber Astronomiae, Part III*, R. Hand, trans., (Berkeley Springs, WV. Golden Hind Press, 1996), 69.

4. Al-Biruni, *The Book of Instruction in the Elements of the Art of Astrology*, R. Ramsay Wright, trans., (Ballantrae Press, 1934) 299.

5. Neither Lilly nor Schoener begin the planets' phases with the conjunctions to the Sun. All Greek sources begin and end the sequence from the Sun's beams. Lilly and Schoener, like their contemporaries, discuss and use the standard delineations for cazimi-combust-beams, but they are not mentioned here.

6. Johannes Schoener, *Opusculum Astrologicum*, R. Hand, trans., (Berkeley Springs, WV Golden Hind Press, 1996), 38.

7. Antonio de Montulmo, *On the Judgment of Nativities, Part 2*, R. Hand, trans., (Berkeley Springs, WV Golden Hind Press), 1995, pp. 39, 46.

8. Al-Biruni calls that being "right of the Sun," what the Medievals called "occidental," and being "left of the Sun," what they called "oriental." Al-Biruni, *The Book of Instruction*, p. 298.

9. William Lilly, *Christian Astrology*, Regulus Press, 1984 facsimile, 115.

10. *Ibid.*, 207.

11. *Ibid.*, 337. He then divides configurations into quadrants to give a more specific age.

12. *Ibid.*, 285.

13. *Ibid.*, 563.

14. Although Ptolemy uses zodiacal signs only for their modalities of cardinal, fixed, and mutable (often called "movable, fixed, common," respectively), the later tradition supplements this with qualities. The Aristotelian understanding interpreted the fire triplicity as hot and dry, the earth triplicity as cold and dry, the air triplicity as hot and wet, and the water triplicity as cold and wet.

15. *Ptolemy, Tetrabiblos, Book I*, R. Schmidt, trans., (Berkeley Springs, WV Golden Hind Press, 1994), Ch 4.

16. *Ibid.*, Ch 4.

17. *Ibid.*, Ch 4.

18. The following is from a short work by Aristotle, *On Length of Life:* "We must grasp that the living creature is naturally moist and warm, and that life too is of this nature, whereas old age is cold and dry, and so is a dead body. This is an observed fact. Now the matter of which all things are composed consists of hot and cold, dry and moist. Thus as they grow old they must dry up, and so the moist things must not be easily dried." Loeb Classical Library edition.

19. Ptolemy, *Tetrabiblos, Book III*, R. Schmidt, trans., (Berkeley Springs, WV Golden Hind Press, 1996), 12.

20. Al-Biruni, *The Book of Instruction*, 299.

21. *Ibid.*, 299.

22. *Ibid.*, 299.

23. Paulus Alexandrinus, *Introductory Matters,* R. Schmidt, trans., (Berkeley Springs, WV Golden Hind Press, 1996), 26-28.

24. This, however, was an erroneous idea as any Briton would be happy to tell you. [Ed.]

25. Paulus Alexandrinus, *Introductory Matters,* Ch 14.

26. Montulmo, *On the Judgment of Nativities, Part 2,* 48; and Ptolemy, *Tetrabiblos, Book III,* 57.

27. Ptolemy, *Tetrabiblos, Book III,* 58.

Printed in the United States
201443BV00002B/1-63/A

9 780966 226614